CREATING SELF-ESTEEM

Lynda Field has a degree in sociology and social psychology. She has trained in counselling and psychotherapy, and runs a private practice specializing in both personal and group development. Lynda lives in Cornwall with her husband and three children.

Dedicated to You

Creating Self-Esteem

A PRACTICAL GUIDE
TO REALIZING YOUR TRUE WORTH

Lynda Field

ELEMENT
Shaftesbury, Dorset ● Rockport, Massachusetts
Brisbane, Queensland

© Lynda Field 1993

First published in Great Britain in 1993 by
Element Books Limited
Shaftesbury, Dorset, SP7 8BP

Published in the USA by
Element, Inc.
42 Broadway, Rockport, MA 01966

Published in Australia in 1993 by
Element Books Limited for
Jacaranda Wiley Limited
33 Park Road, Milton, Brisbane 4064

Reprinted December 1993
Reprinted June and December 1994

Cover design by Max Fairbrother
Text design by Roger Lightfoot
Typeset by Poole Typesetting, Bournemouth
Printed and bound in Great Britain by
Redwood Books Limited, Trowbridge, Wiltshire

British Library Cataloguing in Publication
data available

Library of Congress Cataloging in Publication
data available

ISBN 1–85230–421–9

Contents

Acknowledgements

Thank you :

Richard – my husband, who has always believed in me and who helped me to recognize my own self worth. Your love and friendship are the perfect gifts.

Leilah – my daughter, who is brave and loving. You show me determination.

Jack – my eldest son, who has great integrity. Your sunny personality brings me joy.

Alex – my youngest son, who is full of fun and freedom. You help me to see things in new ways.

Barbara and Idwal Goronwy – my parents. You have given me so much.

Mary Field – my mother-in-law. You have always supported me.

Barbara Higham – the best friend in the world. You are always ready to listen.

My clients, colleagues and teachers – you are my continuing source of inspiration.

Julia McCutchen – my editor at Element Books Ltd. Your vision has helped to make this book a reality.

Thank you also to the following publishers for permission to reproduce text from:

Managing Assertively, Madelyn Burley-Allen. Copyright © John Wiley and Sons, 1983. Reprinted by permission of John Wiley and Sons Inc.

A Woman In Your Own Right, Anne Dickson. Copyright © Quartet Books Ltd., 1985.

Pulling Your Own Strings, Dr. Wayne W. Dyer. Copyright © W. W. Dyer 1978. Hamlyn Books, 1979.

About Understanding, Andreas Fuglesang. Copyright © Andreas Fuglesang, 1982. Dag Hammarskjöld Foundation.

Living In the Light, Shakti Gawain. Copyright © Shakti Gawain and Laurel King, 1986. Published by Nataraj Publishing. Published in UK by Eden Grove Editions, 1988.

Remember Be Here Now, Copyright © Hanuman Foundation, 1980.

You Can Heal Your Life, Louise L. Hay. Copyright © Hay House Inc., Carson, CA. 1984. Published in UK by Eden Grove Editions, 1988. Used by permission.

Preface

Trailing clouds of glory do we come.

W. Wordsworth

Look into a baby's eyes and see the joy and delight which can be found there. You were once like this – enchanted by life, open and trusting, at the centre of your own universe. You felt free to express your emotions, you laughed and cried when you wanted to, you deserved to experience all that life had to offer – this was your birthright.

We come full of the miraculous wonder which our life has to offer. We love ourselves, we love the world, we love everybody. We arrive with our sense of self worth intact, we are full of self-esteem.

When you are high in self-esteem you feel good about yourself. You feel in control of your life and you are flexible and resourceful. You enjoy the challenges which life presents and you are always ready to take life head on. You feel powerful and creative and you know how to 'make things happen' in your life. How often do you feel like this?

As our babyhood passes and we learn the ways of the world our clouds of glory float away. We learn self doubt and we learn to be defensive so that we can 'protect' ourselves. As we lose that feeling of trust in ourselves, the world and everybody, so we lose our self-esteem in equal measure.

As a counsellor and therapist, working with people and their problems, I encounter the negative effects of low self-esteem all the time. Some people have such a low sense of self worth that their lifestyles become totally self destructive. Happily, the majority of us don't fall to these depths of hopelessness and negativity; we go up and down, sometimes feeling good about ourselves and sometimes not. When we are feeling 'not so good' our self-esteem is low and we stop believing in ourselves, and it is at this point that our problems begin. If low self-esteem lies at the root of our personal problems then we can change the quality of our lives by working directly on increasing our self-esteem. In the therapeutic process all roads lead to self-esteem.

In nearly all fields of counselling, the development of self-esteem is now recognized as the key factor in positive self development. With the help of my clients I have developed many methods to increase self-esteem and eventually I brought all the techniques together to make this book. Because we are all different, with a unique set of strengths and weaknesses, there are techniques to suit each one of us, whatever the occasion and whatever 'type' of person we are. In whichever area of your life you feel you need support, you will find the necessary tools to help you in this book.

Creating Self-Esteem is all about you. It focuses on your individual ability to create for yourself a strong sense of self worth which, in turn, leads to high self-esteem. You can learn to make decisions; act spontaneously; say 'no' when necessary; enjoy your own company; and express your feelings. You can become a person who 'makes things happen'. Use this book to create buckets full of self-esteem. Re-claim your glory: after all it is your birthright!

Introduction

Self-Esteem – A Balanced Way of Life

It is easy to recognize when someone has high self-esteem. They are enjoying their life to the full; they are able to be what they want to be and do what they want to do.

When we are high in self-esteem we are able to make choices about how we run our lives. We can realize our own potential and we do this by integrating *all* our abilities in a balanced and harmonious way. If we are low in self-esteem then we no longer feel in control of our experiences and our life is out of balance. What does this mean in practical terms? How can we become balanced?

Let's look at what is involved each time we have an experience. To each experience we bring our whole self and we integrate all our faculties. This 'holistic' approach describes us as existing simultaneously at the spiritual, mental, emotional and physical levels. This simply means that we bring *all* aspects of our 'humanness' to each of our experiences. Figure 1 shows how this works.

Imagine that you are meeting a friend. You bring your spiritual, mental, emotional and physical energy to this encounter. You bring a spiritual experience of your own inner awareness, your *connection* with the life force. You *understand* the encounter with your mental energy. Your emotional energy allows you to have *feelings* about what is

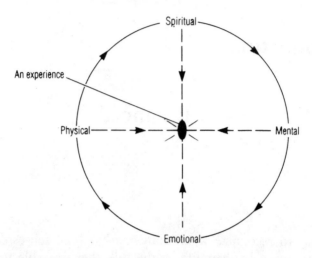

Figure 1   *The holistic nature of an experience*

going on and your physical energy enables you to play an *active* part in this interaction. Figure 2 shows how each 'type' of energy allows us a different 'type' of experience.

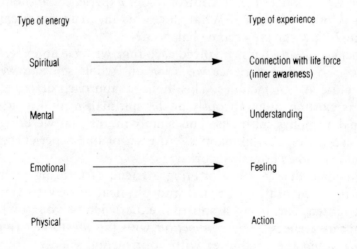

Figure 2   *Energy levels and experience*

When we combine the 'types' of energy which we use at each level of our being we are able to have a whole, well balanced experience. Our spiritual, mental, emotional and physical elements are interactive; they affect each other and are mutually dependent. When I speak of 'levels' I am only talking about the different ways which we have of experiencing. We are able to connect, feel, understand and act. The experience of interaction is multi-dimensional.

This explains *how* we have an experience, but how do we affect its quality? For optimum quality we need a balanced interaction between mind, body, spirit and emotions. When our activity is balanced we can create a lifestyle which supports our self-esteem.

As we all know, experiences can be good or bad. Throughout this book a good experience is described as 'creative' and is linked with high self-esteem. A bad experience is called a 'victim' experience and is linked with low self-esteem. There is only one difference between a victim experience and a creative experience and that lies in the *way* in which our spiritual, mental, emotional and physical energies are integrated. If these energies are in balance our experience is creative; if they are out of balance we will be victims (see Figures 3 and 4).

What sort of experiences are you having?

You are a victim if you feel that you have no choices. You feel uncomfortable and out of control in your life. Things 'just happen' to you (or don't). You are low in self-esteem and you don't feel good.

If you are a creative person you feel at ease and you are able to 'make things happen'. You create your own experiences and so feel in control of your destiny. You are high in self-esteem and you feel good!

Creativity is here defined as the coming together of spiritual, emotional, mental and physical energies in a *balanced* way.

Figure 4 represents the harmonious movement of freely flowing energy, drawing on the universal source (by way of

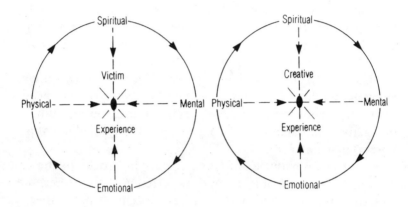

Figure 3   *A victim experience*   Figure 4   *A creative experience*

our spiritual connection) and expressing itself through us, mentally, emotionally, spiritually and physically in a balanced and satisfying way. This is true creative energy.

What is it like to experience such a movement of energy? Some often-used descriptions are that it feels – real / focused / centred / connected / empowering / high / exciting / mentally exhilarating / physically satisfying. Perhaps you have other ways of expressing this feeling.

Creative responses support self-esteem which further encourages creative behaviour. When we are responding creatively we are acting from a state of *creative consciousness*.

Victim-type reactions are similarly self reinforcing because they support low self-esteem which promotes further victim behaviour. When we are responding as victims we are acting from a state of *victim consciousness*.

'Cycles of consciousness' (Figure 5) shows just how these two different states of consciousness affect the quality of our lives. If you operate with creative consciousness you are valuing yourself for what you *are* and not just for what you do. Your sense of self worth does not depend upon you having a high-profile job or earning a lot of money or being clever. Self worth has nothing to do with job status or IQ or never getting things wrong. In other words you are not worth less (worthless) if you can't do something or you make a mistake. This idea of *intrinsic self worth* is the belief on which all self-esteem is based.

A positive self belief encourages an expansive world view which enhances the quality of our lives. This view of the world is one which allows for the creative experience of choice. We are free to initiate change and so can enjoy an action-based lifestyle in which we are able to communicate our needs clearly. Such behaviour supports our feeling of self worth – it reinforces our self-esteem.

If you operate from a state of victim consciousness your lack of positive self belief is strengthened in a similar manner. Without a sense of intrinsic self worth you have a limited world view which provides you with little or no choice. Such a belief creates a reactive lifestyle in which you are always looking for the approval of others before you can act. Figure 5 shows how such a fear-based lifestyle results in unclear communication and consequent feelings of resentment, anger and blame. Hence the victim's lack of self-esteem is reinforced.

Whenever you operate with low self-esteem you have allowed yourself to become a victim. This happens when your life is out of balance.

Experiences can change. You can be acting from creative consciousness, having a good experience and feeling high in self-esteem when unexpectedly everything changes. Something happens and you react badly, you no longer feel high

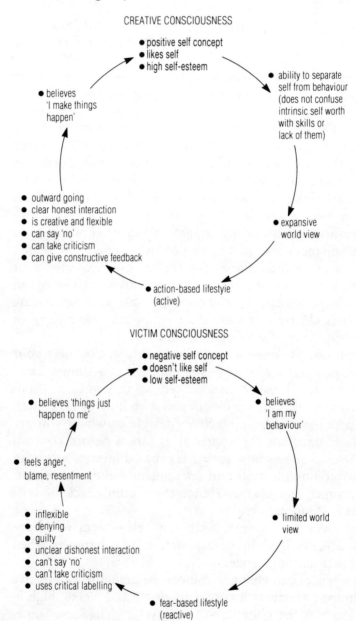

Figure 5   *Cycles of consciousness*

in self-esteem, you respond as a victim and you have a bad experience. This is an uncomfortable sensation because you feel out of control and unsure about what is happening. We all know only too well how this feels – our self-esteem is on the line and we panic! When this happens our spiritual, mental, emotional and physical energies are not integrating – our experiences of *connecting, understanding, feeling* and *acting* are not in harmony. Somewhere our energy is blocked and we are are out of balance.

Can you think of a time when you were feeling good and everything was going fine and then suddenly you found yourself unable to cope? What caused this sudden change in your feelings? Why couldn't you deal with the situation? Where was your energy blocked?

This book will help you to discover your own personal energy blocks. These blocks can occur at any of our 'levels' of experience and of course will affect the quality of our 'whole' experience. If our energy is blocked anywhere in our *connecting, understanding, feeling* or *action* then we are out of balance and this means that we become victims, with low self-esteem.

There are as many ways of changing as there are people. Each of us is unique with our own special abilities and our own individual difficulties.

Maybe you know how to 'look inside' and can feel relaxed but don't know how to bring this experience into a material reality. In other words you can *connect* but can't *act* upon this connection – you can imagine and be inspired but cannot put this into effect.

Perhaps you can *act* in a fairly spontaneous way but do not feel that there is any more to your life than that which appears in front of your eyes – a 'what else is there?' sort of feeling. In this case you are finding it difficult to *connect*.

You may be very emotionally aware and sensitive to other people's feelings. If so, you are in touch with your own *feelings*, but does this gift work for you? Do you know how to stop yourself from being so overwhelmed by emotion that you are unable to *act*?

Possibly you are very good at *understanding* ideas but they stay in your head and you aren't able to *act* upon them, or perhaps you find it difficult to have an experience beyond that of the mind.

Balance is the key to creativity and when we operate with creative consciousness we are high in self-esteem. This book is designed to show you how to create high self-esteem. The method it uses is that of re-balancing your energies by the means of simple techniques. Once you discover where you have a block you can use the appropriate technique to unblock your energy.

It is possible to change whatever 'type' of person you think you are!

The book is divided into four sections which are based on the four 'levels' of awareness which we bring to each of our experiences: Part 1 Connecting (spiritual experience); Part 2 Understanding (mental experience); Part 3 Feeling (emotional experience); and Part 4 Acting (physical experience).

Of course connecting, understanding, feeling and acting are not really separate; they are interdependent and so they help to create each other. However, for the purposes of finding our blocks and freeing them, we need to separate these activities in some way.

Each of the four sections involves reader participation. This book is about you. It is tailor made for your requirements, but you must become involved. This will mean that *you* decide where you need to make changes. *You* evaluate your own answers to the questionnaires and then decide which techniques to use. It is an exciting process and you will feel yourself changing.

You are a creative being. Go ahead and create your self-esteem. Enjoy this book.

Part 1

Connecting

Fix thy soul's gaze upon the star whose rays thou art, the flaming star that shines within the lightless depths of ever-being.

Madame Blavatsky

1.

Your Spiritual Self

There is sometimes a tendency for us to see our material and spiritual 'selves' as being separate, or even in conflict with each other. Of course we need both 'parts'. Our material form would be only a dead body without our spirit (life force) and obviously our spirit would be unable to be part of the physical world without a body. Our spiritual self expresses itself through our material form. The traditional spiritual path is one of retreat, withdrawing from the 'diversions' offered by the material world to concentrate on one's own inner life. But we don't need to live a monastic existence to develop our self awareness; indeed it is preferable that we don't. When we can harmonize our spiritual awareness with our material desires (and the limitations imposed by the physical form), we are living a balanced life; we have developed a creative consciousness and we are high in self-esteem.

Have you ever felt inspired to act – perhaps to make or do something? There is an extraordinary rush of energy and clarity which accompanies such inspirations. You feel excited, can't wait to begin the project, and everything seems possible. Putting the dream into effect can be a sobering process.

My son had a 'brilliant idea' (his words). He came to me

full of excitement and enthusiasm. 'I'm going to make a puppet theatre mum. I know how I'm going to do it, I need some wood and a few nails . . . and I'm going to make the curtains out of that red material . . . and I'm going to make string puppets and make the legs in two parts and drill holes in the wood to join the bits so that the knees will bend' . . . and so on. Such clarity of vision: eyes sparkling, excitement. Half an hour later he went out to play football. I asked what had happened to his project. 'Oh well, I couldn't get the wood to fit together properly and it took ages to saw the lengths and one bit was too long.' The pieces of wood are still under his bed.

We are looking here at what Shakti Gawain calls the 'discrepancy' between our spirit and our form:

> The spirit is very powerful and creative and has a lot of things it would like to do to express itself in the physical world, but it needs to have the form as a vehicle in which to do it. The form is willing but isn't yet able to go where the spirit wants to go. It has to be educated and transformed through the power and the wisdom of the spirit.
>
> Shakti Gawain, *Living In The Light*

In spirit we move at the speed of light – our consciousness has wings. Have you ever experienced a new understanding and awareness only to find that you have lost the feeling soon after? Where did this insight go and why couldn't you hold on to it? The experience of the new perspective is still with you but you just can't see it any more. If we fall back into habitual, limiting thought and behaviour patterns our new perspective is obscured. As we work consistently on our inner awareness (our spiritual self) the changes permeate our form (mind/body/personality). When this happens our spiritual, mental, emotional and physical selves are integrated and we can experience our creative potential – we can 'make things happen' and our self-esteem is high.

When you are developing your spiritual self you learn to

trust your intuitive awareness. This awareness produces a clarity of thought which illuminates the areas where you have created blocks to your freely flowing energy – it throws light on patterns of behaviour which are now inappropriate. You will begin to see both *where* and *how* you need to change. Your physical actions will thus be transformed by your increasing trust in yourself. It will become easy to make decisions and to act spontaneously and this will mean that you will become more effective in your life. Your feeling of self worth will be reinforced and this will be reflected in all areas of your life, including personal relationships, health and work.

Being and Doing

> I contradict myself. I am large. I contain multitudes.
> Walt Whitman

There have been many attempts within psychology to categorize personality 'types'; for example introverted/extraverted, ectomorphic/endomorphic/mesomorphic, sanguine/phlegmatic/choleric. Such categorization may prove self defeating. If I typecast you in a specific way I may have set myself up to *expect* a certain type of behaviour from you, and the chances are that you will learn to fulfil that expectation.

Sally worked on the stage. She was in her mid-thirties and had a fast-moving and glamorous lifestyle. When I first met her she said that she had everything going for her – but that she was desperately unhappy. During counselling she revealed that she had never really wanted an acting career. Her mother had been very ambitious for her daughter and had literally pushed her on to the stage – where Sally had been very successful. Sally said, 'It was just as if something was set in motion and I could never stop it, I only ever wanted mummy to be proud of me.' It emerged that Sally had always felt out of place in the theatrical set. She had to make a great effort in order to fulfil the requirements of her image: 'I am not really a gregarious, theatrical type but I know how to act out what is expected of me. It has taken me a long time to realize that I have been fulfilling the expectations of others, firstly those of my mother and then those of my audiences.' Sally was only able to address this issue after her mother had died; it was only then that she felt free to look at her own feelings. She eventually left the theatre at the height of her career and went to university to study philosophy. She seemed a shy and easily intimidated sort of person but that is not how her colleagues and her audience had seen her.

To typify can be dangerous and so maybe we need to look in a broader way at personality 'types'. We could describe our lives as encompassing the states of *doing* and *being*:

- *Doing* describes activity *out* in the world
- *Being* describes awareness *within* the person.

Figure 6 shows how high self-esteem is related to activity which includes a balanced mixture of being and doing. Doing and being complement each other and are inseparable. However, some people are largely doers and others are be-ers. You may possibly be a be-er in some areas of your life whilst being a doer in other areas. The centre of Figure 6 represents a balanced mixure of 'inner' and 'outer' activity. If you are operating in this central area you are not afraid to go out into the world but you also know when to stop and look 'inside' at your own requirements. Your energy is freely flowing and you are 'at ease' with yourself. Some people will be primarily doers or be-ers in all areas of their lives whilst most will be a combination of the two – exhibiting differing patterns of behaviour in different parts of their lives.

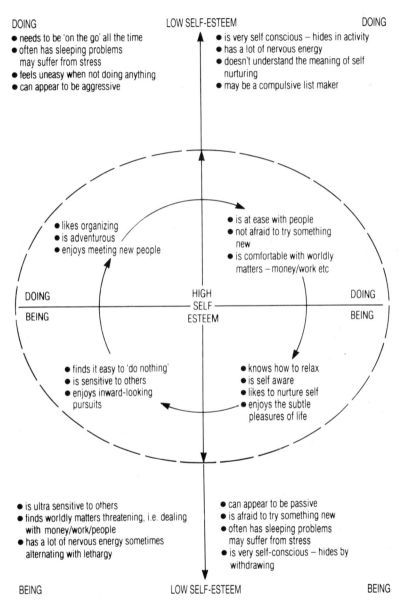

DOING
- needs to be 'on the go' all the time
- often has sleeping problems
  may suffer from stress
- feels uneasy when not doing anything
- can appear to be aggressive

LOW SELF-ESTEEM

DOING
- is very self conscious – hides in activity
- has a lot of nervous energy
- doesn't understand the meaning of self nurturing
- may be a compulsive list maker

- likes organizing
- is adventurous
- enjoys meeting new people

- is at ease with people
- not afraid to try something new
- is comfortable with worldly matters – money/work etc

DOING
BEING

HIGH
SELF
ESTEEM

DOING
BEING

- finds it easy to 'do nothing'
- is sensitive to others
- enjoys inward-looking pursuits

- knows how to relax
- is self aware
- likes to nurture self
- enjoys the subtle pleasures of life

- is ultra sensitive to others
- finds worldly matters threatening, i.e. dealing with money/work/people
- has a lot of nervous energy sometimes alternating with lethargy

- can appear to be passive
- is afraid to try something new
- often has sleeping problems
  may suffer from stress
- is very self-conscious – hides by withdrawing

BEING

LOW SELF-ESTEEM

BEING

Figure 6 *Being and doing*

As we move away from the centre of the diagram we can see the dangers inherent at each end of the spectrum. At the complete extremes we see super self-conscious people, in other words those with very low self-esteem, *hiding* either in frantic activity or in withdrawal.

Do you recognize any of the personality traits shown in the diagram? Do any of them apply to you? Imagine yourself in the following situations.

- You are at a party and you don't know anyone except the hostess.

  How do you feel? .... How do you act?...................

- You have returned an article of clothing which has split along a seam. The shop assistant tells you that the company has a 'no returns' policy.

  How do you feel? .... How do you act?...................

- A doctor is not answering your questions satisfactorily; (s)he is being evasive.

  How do you feel............... How do you act?...................

Which way do you tend to go when under pressure? How do you react in a potentially threatening situation?

When our behaviour out in the world expresses our true feelings, then our being and doing are in balance; we are being true to ourselves and we are high in self-esteem.

2.

Nurturing Yourself

'Enjoy yourself.' We use this phrase over and over again but are we always aware of its true meaning? Do you know how to do it? Before you can enjoy yourself you need to *know* your 'self'. In order to learn about yourself, *you need to be selfish*.

How do you react to this statement? Some common responses include:

- Selfish people aren't nice.
- I was always told not to be selfish and to share my things.
- Selfish people take advantage of others.
- I was taught to think always of others first.

The Collins English dictionary defines 'selfish' as '(1) chiefly concerned with one's own interest, advantage etc esp. to the total exclusion of the interests of others, (2) relating to or characterized by self interest'. Sometimes it is totally appropriate to be 'self'ish. I am asking you to be chiefly concerned with your own interests *especially* to the exclusion of the interests of others. You cannot truly discover your 'self' if you are always putting the interests of others first. Perhaps you need to give yourself permission to nurture yourself. Try to set aside some time every day, even if it is only a few minutes, to think solely about your own needs.

'I deserve to devote time exclusively to my own needs.'
How do you feel when you say this? Some of the replies I
have heard include:

- But what about everyone else?
- I don't know if I'm really worth it.
- People might not like me if I put my self first.
- I feel silly.
- I'm afraid of what this might mean.
- Great, how do I go about getting it?

I Wanna Walk Like You And Even Talk Like You

In order to make our material world 'safe', 'secure' and
'knowable' we have created institutions and standardized
behaviour patterns which support the status quo. This is
how we try to make some sense of our world, and of course
there is a need to objectify our reality in some way, but
remember that excessive conformity is a trap from which
the spirit cannot fly.

> It takes a great deal of self confidence for people to consult
> their internal resources to determine what they want to do,
> and when people don't have that self-esteem, they use the
> only other standards available – comparisons with others,
> which virtually everyone is willing to use, because they are so
> effective at keeping folks in line.
> Dr Wayne W. Dyer, *Pulling Your Own Strings*

Dr Dyer talks about the phenomenon of 'constant comparison shopping'. I think that this beautifully describes the way
we often 'buy into' the concept of a comparative scale of self
worth. There is a tenuous but false security available when
we look for models outside ourselves. We can be tempted by
the luxury of limited decision making and wooed by the

myth that if only we use 'so and so' product we too will look as elegant / be as confident / sound as intelligent . . . as whom? Do you ever compare yourself with others? How do you know if you are clever / worthy / confident / beautiful / happy / doing well / doing badly . . . etc? No one else can be inside you. No one else can experience your self satisfaction (or your lack of it). Only you know what it feels like to be you. If you look outside yourself to find an oracle of comparison you are effectively denying your own decision-making powers and in doing so you disown your unique inheritance – your own special place in this world. Every time you compare yourself with someone else you are mistrusting your own ability to make appropriate choices. You are operating from a state of victim consciousness and your self-esteem is low and still falling.

Everywhere I Go There I Am

'*I am unique.*' How do you feel when you make this statement? Every single one of us is unique and wherever we go we take our individual specialness. Why do we often find it so difficult to see ourselves in this way?

Look at a flower seed display. There are so many different types of seed. Some seeds are grown at one time of the year, another type at another time. They need different types of soil / sun / shade conditions. There are so many variable needs involved. Even if you plant only one type of seed and all the seeds experience the same conditions, every single flower will be different in some way. As with all living things, each seed needs to be nurtured appropriately to ensure successful flowering.

The first step of your inner journey begins with the idea of self nurturing. This requires that:

- Your consider yourself worthy of attention.
- You are ready to face the fact of your uniqueness.
- You are willing to spend some time exclusively on yourself.

Reflect on the feelings which arose when you read these three statements. By positively affirming the statements, you will immediately begin to break down any resistance you may have to these ideas. Feelings of unworthiness and uncertainty grow from lack of emotional support during early childhood. (We will look at this issue and the use of affirmations in much greater detail in Part 2.) Meanwhile, turn the statements into positive affirmations and say out loud to yourself:

- I . . . (your name) . . . consider myself worthy of attention.
- I . . . am willing to spend some time exclusively on myself.
- I . . . am unique.

Is it difficult to say these things about yourself? Is one more difficult to say than another? Spend some time repeating each statement and note all thoughts and feelings which come up for you. If you experience difficulties whilst doing this activity *please don't give up!* Contradictory thought patterns usually arise. They go something like this: 'Who do I think I am, saying things like this about myself?'/ 'This is too silly; what use is all this anyway?' / 'I really can't afford to waste time on this; I have other things to do'. Maybe you have thought of something else. Whatever happens, don't stop saying these affirmations out loud to yourself until you feel ready to take on your self nurturing. Such contradictory thought patterns, which erode your self-esteem, point to the areas where you find it difficult to accept your own self worth. You cannot begin your inner journey until you believe that you deserve to be nurtured!

The inner journey of self awareness is very personal. No one else travels on your particular path although others may travel alongside you at different times. No one else can find your path, only you! If you find your path blocked at any time only you can clear it. *You are your own roadsweeper!* If you don't keep clearing your path it will become chock-a-block with debris and you will be stuck, unable to move any further. When you feel stuck in any situation and you can't move forward it means that your energy is being blocked – somewhere in any of the four levels. There are plenty of techniques in this book which will show you how to recognize and how to unblock these personal energy blocks. The usefulness of these techniques is however greatly enhanced by using the process which I have called 'connecting'. When we 'connect' we reach levels of awareness which are far beyond those of conscious thought. At these new levels we learn super-creative ways to deal with problems – ways which our rational mind would have never dreamed possible.

3.

Your Inner Journey

We know how to satisfy our material desires by going out into the world and experiencing it with our body senses and thoughts. But is this enough? The satisfaction of material desires is an elusive state – the more we get the more we want. We will never be totally fulfilled by anything which the material world has to offer because we need nourishment at all levels of our being.

It is very hard to describe the experience of 'connecting'. The closest I can come to a description is to call it a feeling of 'oneness' with the rest of the universe. This feeling of connecting can be activated in many different ways. Times of crisis or even of great change can make things look different; our vision alters somehow as we are pushed beyond our normal sensory experiences. Yoga and Tai Chi are examples of activities which still the mind and can lead us to experience inner changes. Have you ever become totally absorbed by a project / a picture / a piece of music / a landscape (or whatever)? The mind becomes concentrated and still and you feel 'at one'. Some women experience such a change in awareness when they give birth – pulled by the forces of nature to experience being a part of something much greater than themselves – beyond thought, beyond the senses.

Anything can trigger such a 'shift' in awareness – a dream, a memory, an evocative smell, falling in love, being afraid. It is only necessary for our defences to be down (which means that we are holding no preconceived ideas) in order that we can experience something new. It is possible therefore that you have already experienced such a change in your awareness.

Can you remember having an experience of connecting? If so, try to recall the feeling.

It is very difficult to describe this feeling of being connected – sometimes words are so inadequate. The rest of this section describes easy techniques which will enable you to make your own personal spiritual connection. All that is required is an open mind.

Open Minds Open Hearts

We have been taught and encouraged to make sense of our universe by categorizing and compartmentalizing – by separating things in order to understand them. To experience connection rather than separation, we need to break all attachments with our thoughts and desires and so learn to suspend our judgement. It is not so much a question of looking for the place beyond our mind but more a question of stopping having views about things.

In order to focus within it is necessary to withdraw a little from our worldly lives. However, it is possible to connect at any time, whatever you are doing. We can meditate in order to make a spiritual connection but we can also experience our spiritual self in the middle of a busy supermarket.

Look back to Figure 5 on page xvi and you can see that if you are a victim, with low self-esteem, you believe that your worth depends upon your abilities. If you make a mistake then you are worthless. This view implies that our worth is only measurable in material terms. However, if you are creating your own experiences you have high self-esteem and do not consider that you *are* your behaviour; your intrinsic sense of self worth does not depend on your successes or lack of them. Intrinsic self worth is the backbone of self-esteem. It disassociates self from doer: we are so much more than the sum of our successes and failures.

How then can we learn to suspend our judgement whilst going about our daily business in the world? Is it possible to withdraw and yet still be involved at a practical level? Can you really have a spiritual experience in the supermarket? The answer is definitely 'yes'.

Self Remembering and the Witness

A long time ago when I began to wonder about the nature of my own spirituality I came across a fantastic technique which was both practical and mind expanding at the same time. George Gurdjieff created this technique which he called *'self remembering'* and he introduced the concept of the 'witness'. The technique appealed to me because it was immediately useful and I didn't have to sit quietly on my own to achieve a spiritual insight. Nowadays I enjoy solitary reflection but I also use self remembering because I can do it anywhere; it is effective, protective and private.

How many 'yous' are there inside you? By lunchtime today I have been – happy / hungry / thoughtful / serious / annoyed / energetic / tired / silly . . . and those are just the ones I can remember. We play many parts throughout the day and who 'you' are changes at every moment (see Figure 7). If we reflect on these numerous 'yous' it becomes possible to devalue their importance. We can often let

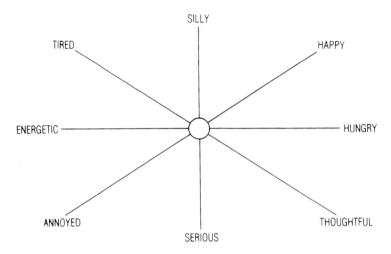

Figure 7   *How many 'yous' are there inside you?*

ourselves 'off the hook' by diminishing the power that we give to these transitory 'you' states. Gurdjieff points out that sometimes one 'you' does something for which every other 'you' must pay, maybe for the rest of your life. Our 'yous' are numerous and ephemeral and all are evaluative and judgemental. To break this identity with our own thoughts is to give ourselves some inner freedom. Can you remember doing something for which you cannot forgive yourself? Perhaps you said something out of place or made some other mistake and still feel guilty and full of self blame. These feelings perpetuate low self-esteem; they serve no effective purpose other than maintaining your victim status. How harshly we judge ourselves, how critical we are of our own endeavours. Do we need to take ourselves so seriously, or can we give ourselves a break?

When we use self remembering we adopt the role of witness as we go about our everyday lives. The witness observes all your doings but is non-evaluative; it does not judge your actions. For example, you may eat a cream cake (an act of desire) and then get annoyed with yourself for having eaten it. The witness (when it arrives) would note:

1. She is eating a cream cake.
2. She is annoyed with herself for eating a cream cake.

The witness is dispassionate and does not care what you do, it merely makes a note of what you do. The following description is a beautiful example of witnessing, taken from the book *Remember Be Here Now*:

> You are walking down a street witnessing yourself walking down a street. You feel happy and witness feeling happy . . . and so it goes. Then you meet someone or see something that irritates you. Immediately you get irritated and forget all about the witness. The adrenalin pumps through you and you think angry thoughts. At this point 'angry me' is who you are. Only *much* later do you remember that you were attempting to witness.
>
>   At that point you promise yourself that you won't forget again. Ah, how little you know about the subtleties of the seductions of the other 'yous'. Again you are walking and again witnessing walking and so forth. This time you meet with another situation which irritates you. Again you lose your witness (or centre as it is called sometimes) and again your endocrine glands secrete and you think angry thoughts. But this time right in the middle of the entire drama you 'wake up'. . . That is, you realise your predicament. But at this point it is difficult to get free of the 'angry you' because you are already getting much gratification. (It's a bit like trying to stop in the midst of a sexual act.)

At first, then, you will probably only remember to witness when you are feeling particularly calm and uninvolved; it will be easy to forget when you get hooked by your emotions. With practice it becomes easier and easier not to forget.

   Practising witnessing, forgetting to witness and then

remembering again can be great fun. It is an entirely private affair and it adds an incredible dimension to everyday life – it adds spice to the most mundane of tasks.

Put down the book and practise witnessing for the next ten minutes. What happened? How often did you forget and then remember again? What made you forget? Was it hard? Did you enjoy it?

The more you use this technique the more powerful it becomes. Each 'you' is a reflection of a link with a desire, feeling or thought – these are our links with the material world. By taking on the role of witness we can objectify these 'yous' and so break our identification with them. This means that we can rise above our transitory states and so can connect in a truly spiritual way. When we experience our spirituality we recognize our true place in the world and we know that we have our own vital role to play. This feeling of truly belonging creates a sense of worthiness which enhances our self-esteem.

Witnessing may sound like a way of opting out of your life by avoiding your true feelings, a way of keeping calm by not becoming truly involved. In reality the opposite is true: the calm centre of the witness allows us to experience a spiritual state where we can feel truly at the centre of our own lives. We can claim our emotional states without being distracted by them. We can freely enjoy being ourselves as there is no need to live in the shadow of any of our 'yous'. This method of connecting can truly liberate a person who is low in self-esteem.

Try this technique whenever you remember. You have nothing to lose except your negative self beliefs. You may gain a lot. I can guarantee that it will change your perceptions in some way.

Being

As we have seen, connecting is about linking rather than thinking; it's about being rather than doing. If you are predominantly a 'doing' sort of person you may find it hard to imagine the concept of 'being'. Being encompasses a state of inner awareness and if we cannot balance this awareness with our outer activity we will never be high in self-esteem.

The act of being requires that we become more detached from our doing. The more we can withdraw from our worldly pursuits (temporarily of course) the greater the power of our spiritual connection. This act of withdrawing often needs a lot of practice because most of us are so used to excessive activity.

Figure 8 shows the different ways we have of connecting, as we move away from 'doing' in the world to 'being' alone inside ourselves. Outside the circle are our 'doing' activities and as we move away from the circumference towards the middle of the circle we are learning to 'be'.

'Me' Time

How much 'me' time do you have daily? Me time is defined here as time spent absolutely for your own personal enjoyment. This may or may not include other people but it is not *for* other people, you do it for yourself. I asked some people (men and women) about their me time. Some said that they didn't have any and the reasons they gave included

- I don't have time.
- I don't know what I'd do.
- I'd feel too guilty to enjoy it.

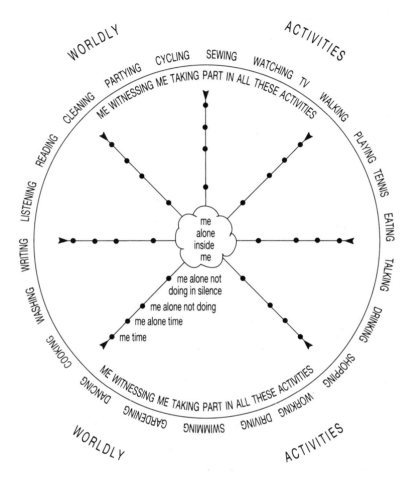

Figure 8 *The connecting process*

Others were doing an enormous range of things in their me time including:

taking a sauna	playing netball	knitting
playing football	swimming	going to the theatre
reading poetry	writing poetry	walking
gardening	playing chess	calligraphy
weight training	photography	having a facial.

There are endless possible ways of spending your me time.

Although these pursuits fall into our category of worldly activities they lead away from the state of 'doing' to the state of 'being' because we are doing them just for ourselves – we are recognizing our own unique needs. The willingness to be self nurturing plays a vital part in the development of our 'beingness'.

Do you have any me time? If not, then why not?

If you have no time to spend on yourself then your self-esteem is very low. You deserve your own personal space – we all do. Taking time out for yourself makes you feel good. Taking me time increases your self-esteem. Your relationship with yourself and others will improve. As you start looking at your own needs and stop playing the victim of other people's demands you will be treated with more respect. Self-esteem is self perpetuating.

It is obviously very important that you make some time for yourself. If you aren't used to spending time alone you may at first find me time absolutely excruciating. Stick with it; it is amazing how pleasant it soon becomes and how enjoyable it feels to be getting to know yourself a bit more.

'Me Alone' Time

Having got used to regular me time you will find it easier to have a go at 'me alone' time. You may have spent some of your me time in solitary pursuits, in which case you have already begun to experience what it feels like to be alone with your thoughts. Some people, who are very low in self-esteem, make a habit of being alone. They spend time alone because they are afraid of worldly activity. Others are terrified to be alone and these people are also low in self-esteem and hide their feelings of inadequacy in excessive 'doing' in the world.

If you are a person with high self-esteem you know how to balance your doing and being activities. You are comfortable with worldly matters and you are also able to 'look inside' and develop your self awareness. Learning to enjoy being alone is an important ingredient of self-esteem.

By the way, such activities as doing the housework, working on the car or watching TV do not count as time spent on 'me alone'. Experiencing 'me alone' requires that anything you 'do' is for your own personal pleasure.

If you are not used to being alone you may need some practice. It may be useful at first to make a note of the details of your 'alone' experiences, to observe what is happening to you and why.

Marlene is twenty-eight and is married with two small children. She told me that she had 'forgotten how to be alone' and that she was afraid of what it would be like. I suggested that she recorded the details of her first week's experiences and you can see the results on page 24.

At the end of the first week Marlene reported that she had found the experience extremely confronting. At first she found it impossible to enjoy being alone. She felt selfish and guilty when she wasn't 'doing' something. It wasn't until the end of the week that she felt comfortable with herself and she said that it was because she was beginning to understand herself a bit more. Me alone time is about getting to know yourself and the more you practise the easier it becomes.

Marlene said that she felt 'like a new woman' and that she had decided to plan her alone time for the following week. Using the same format as before, she structured her time so that she knew beforehand how long she would be

When	Where	How long	What did it feel like?	What did you do?
SUNDAY	At home	30 mins	Quite good but I felt a bit selfish	watched TV although I knew this wasn't a 'me alone' activity
MONDAY			NO TIME ALONE	
TUESDAY	In the garden	2 hours	I felt that I had achieved something	weeding hedge-cutting
WEDNESDAY	At home	Not long	Hassled by the rest of the family	reading
THURSDAY	In the park	20 mins	Good to get out of the house but couldn't stop thinking about what I had to do at home	Walked the dog
FRIDAY	At home	40 mins	Terrible – I felt so guilty	Fell asleep
SATURDAY	At home	about 1 hour	I enjoyed myself!	Put my feet up

Table 1   *Marlene's 'me alone' table*

alone and where she would be. Initially Marlene also felt the need to know beforehand *what* she would be doing. However, by the end of the second week she felt so much more at ease in her own company that she dropped her plans of what to do in favour of what she called 'spontaneous happenings'.

If being alone is a new experience for you, these methods of observing and structuring may prove very supportive. Use whichever techniques are helpful until you no longer need them. When you are enjoying your me alone time you have truly learned the meaning of enjoying your self.

Do you remember how it felt to say 'I deserve to devote time exclusively to my own needs'? How does it feel when you say that now?

Your feelings about yourself, your self-esteem or lack of it, depend on whether you can be self nurturing. You are a very special person with your own unique connection with the universe. Discover and enjoy your own amazingness.

We are learning to cut our worldly ties in order to experience something which is beyond the realms of our everyday activity. We are approaching a state of 'not doing', but first we need to know how to be alone with ourself.

'Me Alone Not Doing' Time

Help!! Yes it's true, you are alone and you are not doing anything. Yes but what can you do? Alone with your thoughts. What a revelation, the power of the mind, the incessant chattering of that inner voice. A session of 'me alone not doing' is often far from peaceful and perhaps that is why so few people do it.

What does it feel like? Try it for five minutes a day for a week. Then try ten minutes a day for the next week. What happened to you? Was it easy or was it hard?

Being alone and not doing is an art in itself. People rarely find it simple at first. The art needs to be learned and happily there are techniques to help. Before we can completely let go of our doingness in order to connect with our beingness we need to focus the mind.

'Me Alone Not Doing In Silence' Time

Stage 1 – The mind is a hard task master

When we are being alone, not doing, in silence, it is helpful to find a comfortable position and to close our eyes. This may be difficult at first. Marlene had to keep her eyes open for the first ten days of trying this exercise because she felt dizzy and afraid when she closed them.

This is Marlene's description of her first experience with this exercise:

> I sat down in a comfortable chair but I couldn't close my eyes so at first I was a bit distracted by things that I could see. Then I became aware of the silence and it felt overpowering and I know it sounds stupid but it seemed like the silence was so loud it was almost too much. And then my mind started talking away about this and that and the other so I tried to silence my mind with my mind saying things like – I must be quiet, I must stop thinking about this. Before I knew it I was getting really angry with myself. I thought that this was supposed to make me feel more peaceful!

Marlene was pretty angry after being alone, not doing in silence for five minutes. She was definitely stirred up by the exercise and far from tranquil. This type of initial experience is predictable. At this stage of connecting we are trying to make a direct link between our own spiritual energy and the energy of the universe – all our distracting structures have been removed and we are alone in our beingness. Small wonder that Marlene was a bit shaken.

At this stage of trying to 'go inside' many people give up – 'I can't do it' . . . 'It's too difficult' . . . 'It upsets me'. This realization of the incredible power of the mind is very important and is really the first stage of learning to experience 'me alone inside me'. Instead of giving up at this point, recognize this as a necessary first step to complete awareness of your spiritual self.

Stage 2 – The mind is a willing servant

Going inside ourselves requires that we break our identification with our worldly links – we are going beyond our thoughts / feelings / desires. To do this we need to focus our attention on something else so that we don't keep thinking about this and that, and then think that we musn't think it.

Understand that the mind will keep on chattering and don't try to stop it.

Here are two techniques which will help you to transcend your mental chatter. Try this first one for ten minutes a day for a week:

Sit comfortably with your eyes closed (if possible). In this way you remove all external distractions. Watch your mind at work, just let it wander. Bring in the witness to observe your thoughts and then to let go of them. Those thoughts will just keep on coming, so don't try to stop them. If you get hooked by a thought you will eventually recognize what you are doing and your witness can note what has happened and then let go.

When this practice becomes familiar you will be able to sit for longer periods:

Sit as before and let your mind wander. Concentrate on the rhythm of your breathing. Follow your in-breath and then your out-breath. Be aware of your breath. As you breathe in think 'in' and as you breathe out think 'out'. So, in, out, in, out. Each time your mind wanders off, follow it, observe that it has wandered and then come back to your breathing. In, out, in, out. Become aware of the place *between* the breaths – when you are not breathing in and you are not breathing out. Now concentrate on this place. Keep watching your breath but move your awareness to this place between the in- and out-breath. When your mind wanders off, follow it and then come back to your in- and out-breaths. Follow the in-breath and then the out-breath until you have regained a comfortable rhythm. Now return your concentration to the place between the breaths.

Going inside requires practice. If it's hard for you, please don't give up. Each time you try it gets a little easier. As you practise, your mind becomes more concentrated. Your spiritual connection is your own link with the universe. Your experiences are totally private and unique and the ability to make this link is extremely valuable. You can cultivate a place, alone inside yourself, where you can go to experience the freedom of your spirit. This place offers a complete break from our worldly activities and after only ten minutes you can feel totally refreshed and invigorated.

When you are consciously nourishing your spiritual self you are reinforcing your feelings of self worth. You cannot balance your being and doing unless you know how to 'be'. You cannot create your own experiences unless you can balance yourself at all levels of your being and one of these levels is connecting.

Part 2

Understanding

No one can be myself like I can. For this job I'm the best
man.

Chesney Hawkes, No. 1 in pop charts March 1991

4.

Changing Your Mind

I am . . . Why am I? I should . . . Why should I? I could . . . change!
How would you describe yourself?

I Am

Look at the adjectives below. Put 'I am' in front of each of them and score as follows: 0 almost never, 1 sometimes, 2 often, 3 almost always.

0 deserving	1 embarrassed	3 unique	0 artistic
1 supportive	2 withdrawn	1 clever	2 sarcastic
1 flexible	2 lazy	1 demanding	2 incapable
2 thoughtful	2 tolerant	0 active	1 kind
1 likeable	2 frightened	2 angry	3 shy
0 exciting	1 happy	1 lighthearted	1 overbearing
1 intelligent	0 loveable	1 proud	2 boring
1 inarticulate	2 responsible	1 depressed	2 sloppy
1 intolerant	1 creative	0 responsive	1 modest
1 tactful	2 passive	1 self aware	0 interesting
2 perceptive	1 confident	1 aggressive	1 unfair
2 uncertain	2 emotional	1 manipulative	2 worried
2 mistrusting	1 enthusiastic	2 sensitive	0 self righteous
1 worthless	2 useless	2 stupid	

We are all of these things some of the time of course, but look particularly at where you scored 0 or 3.

Write down all the things that you think you are almost never.

I am almost never .... *self righteous   artistic* ....
.... *responsive   active ~~liveable~~* ....
.... *exciting   deserving   interesting* ....

Now all those things which you believe you are almost always.

I am almost always .... *unique   shy* ....
....

Are there any descriptions that you would like to add? If so put them on your lists.

Write down the three adjectives which you believe best describe you, whether from this list or your own.

I am .... *uncertain   mistrusting   useless   sloppy* ....
I am .... *sometimes   clever   sensitive   kind* ....
I am .... *sincere* ....

Which of these statements do you consider the most important? This is your underlying personal self belief, what I call your *core belief*. What does your core belief reveal about you? How do you see yourself? Is your core belief appreciative or critical; in other words, are you high or low in self-esteem?

If you have a poor self image (and most people have) look again at all the words that you have used to describe yourself. Imagine that you are saying such things about another person. Would you be so hard and judgemental with someone else? Remember that you are describing yourself. How would you feel if someone else described you in this way?

If your core belief is a negative one (and I expect that it is) look carefully at it again. Core beliefs follow a recognizable pattern:

- They are extremely self critical.
- They often contain words such as worthless / useless / too
  ... (something or other).
- They are irrational.
- They perpetuate low self-esteem.

Look back at the exercise which you have just done. What a list of negative beliefs! Where have they all come from?

Louise Hay, in her wonderful book, *You Can Heal Your Life*, suggests a way which helps to pinpoint the source(s) of our limiting beliefs about self. It requires that you make an 'I should' list.

I Should

Write down all the things you think that you should do.

I should ....

....

....

Give yourself a ten minute time limit here or you might be at it for hours.

This is a (shortened) should list belonging to a client, called Rose, who has kindly allowed me to use it as an example.

I *should* read a lot more.
I *should* like my job.
I *should* be nicer to people.
I *should* love my sister.
I *should* lose weight.
I *should* be more interesting.
I *should* get up earlier in the morning.
I *should* love my mother.

Why Should I?

Take each 'I should', read it out loud and then ask yourself 'why should I?' Speaking out loud to yourself in this way makes the technique more effective. Voicing your feelings can help your understanding. Write down your answers. You may be surprised by what you have written.

Here are a few examples of some typical answers to the 'why should I' question:

- Because everybody has to do it.
- My father said I should.
- What will happen to me if I don't?
- Because people won't like me anymore.
- Because I'm too fat / stupid / lazy / thin / worthless / careless etc.

The answers to 'why should I' questions show us how we can limit ourselves by holding certain beliefs. Try ending an 'I should' statement with 'because I really want to'. The sentence doesn't make sense because the word 'should' implies reluctance. Its use also indicates feelings of guilt and fear. Do we really need to burden ourselves in this way?

Every time you think that you 'should' or 'ought to' do something, stop and examine what meaning such thoughts really hold for you. Louise Hay puts it like this:

. . . I believe that should is one of the most damaging words in our language. Every time we use should we are in effect saying 'wrong'. Either we *are* wrong or we *were* wrong or we are *going to be wrong*. I don't think we need more wrongs in our life. We need more freedom of choice. I would like to take the word SHOULD and remove it from the vocabulary forever. I replace it with the word COULD. Could gives us choice and we are never wrong.

I Could

So what happens when you do as Ms Hay suggests and you change your should list, replacing should with could, and start each statement with, 'If I really wanted to'? This is what Rose's list looked like:

If I really wanted to I could read a lot more.
If I really wanted to I could like my job.
If I really wanted to I could be nicer to people.
If I really wanted to I could love my sister.
If I really wanted to I could lose weight.
If I really wanted to I could be more interesting.
If I really wanted to I could get up earlier in the morning.
If I really wanted to I could love my mother.

After changing her list in this way Rose said, '. . . somehow things seem much more possible. I looked at that should list and I really didn't know where to start. The idea of actually doing any of those things was so daunting, each should felt like a heavy burden. When I changed the list I couldn't believe how different I felt. For a start there are some things I didn't even want to change! I don't really want to read a lot more, I'm quite happy reading things which interest me. I don't understand where I got that idea from. I don't really want to like my job, it's so boring. What I really want is to change my job but I'm afraid to try . . .' and so it went on. Rose was able to stop blaming herself for anything and everything and begin a more constructive approach to her life. When she realized that she no longer needed to be a victim of what she thought she 'should' be doing, she began to respond creatively and her self-esteem increased accordingly.

How is your 'I could' list looking? Is there anything on this list which you can abandon? You may have been criticizing yourself for not doing something which you had no wish to do in the first place. Rose discovered why she had questioned her reading habits when she heard her father say to her daughter, 'You should read a lot more'. Rose said that she felt that she now 'heard' this message in a different way. She said '. . . I had just forgotten how many times my father had said that to me. I suppose it's a bit like listening to the same tape over and over again. In the end you don't listen to it any more but you know it off by heart.'

We learn many important messages 'by heart' when we are very young and these can have a powerful effect in our adult life! If you are hanging on to inappropriate messages you can learn to *let go* of them! Give yourself permission to run your own life. You can make your own decisions and create your own experiences. If your core belief is negative then your self concept will be poor and your self-esteem will be low. If your core belief is positive your self concept will be good and your self-esteem will be high. Negative beliefs about yourself undermine your feelings of self worth – let go of these beliefs and go for self-esteem!

I Could Change

Is there anything on your 'I could' list which you feel that you would like to tackle. Why haven't you? Do you feel too afraid to try? Do you feel unable to try?

The rationale which supports 'I should' (and 'I should not') allows us to hand over the responsibility for our lives to others. Whenever you say 'I should . . . .' you take a childlike stance and give away your decision-making power to someone else. The 'should' habit inhibits change, risk taking and assertive behaviour. It is both comforting and severely limiting. Whenever we question our basic beliefs we are questioning our status quo and this may feel very threatening.

Rose decided that she did want to lose weight but she said, 'I feel totally unable to start becaue I'm not disciplined enough and I'm just too sloppy and untogether'. We limit our ability to change our lives when we subscribe to the belief that we are 'not good enough' in some way or that we are 'too' something or other. Are such thought patterns restricting your life in any way? There is no need to judge yourself in this way – there are no standards of comparison. You are unique.

Look again at your core belief – do you still believe it?

We Are What We Believe We Are

We have learned our beliefs about ourselves at a very early age. As young children we can only make sense of ourselves and of the world through interpretation by the important adult figures in our lives – the most influential of these being, usually, our parents. Our subconscious mind accepts all things literally and so the new, open, trusting and enquiring mind of the small child absorbs, accepts and unquestioningly believes both positive and negative messages.

By taking on negative or positive beliefs about ourselves we can make our own self-fulfilling prophecy. We will prove what we believe to be true about us. How is this possible? The important thing to remember here is that our beliefs are *only* beliefs – they do not have an objective reality. However, if we are determined enough to 'prove' our beliefs we really can. For example if I believe, 'I am a loser' I can bring about some magic and create a situation whereby I truly am always a loser. I can prove to myself that I was right and that I was born to fail!

I go for a job interview. The job sounds interesting and the pay is good. Already I'm thinking that the job is too good for a person like me. I enter the waiting room where there are a lot of other applicants. Oh that's the end, there's no hope for me, just look at the competition, I may as well go home. And I may as well go home! I am perfectly right, I haven't a hope of getting the job. If I go in to the interview believing that I am not good enough for the job then it will not be hard to convince the interviewer that I am unsuitable. At least I will be able to say 'I told you so, I knew I wouldn't get it, I am always unlucky in life'. I will have the questionable satisfaction of being able to blame my victim status, and my low self-esteem will be reinforced.

Happily, we can also use our magic to make our positive beliefs come true.

I hold the belief that, 'I am a lucky person'. I go for the same job. I enter the waiting room and see all the others. I get chatting to some of the applicants – well, I may as well have an interesting afternoon, it looks as though I'm going to be sitting here for a while. The competition looks quite tough but I've as good a chance as anybody. Anyway I've nothing to lose and, knowing my good luck, everything to gain. I may well get the job, which will further prove how lucky I am. However, if I don't get the job it won't disprove my self belief – what had I got to lose by trying – at least I had a go! Most importantly, my self-esteem remains intact.

Figure 9 shows how we can perpetuate and reinforce our self beliefs, and create a self-fulfilling prophecy. Madelyn Burley-Allen (in *Managing Assertively*) describes the power of belief in this way:

> Some of your beliefs originated in your childhood, but you are not at their mercy unless you believe that you are. Because your imagination follows your beliefs, you can find yourself in a vicious circle in which you constantly paint mental pictures that reinforce negative aspects of your life.
>
> The imaginative events generate appropriate emotions, which automatically bring hormonal changes in your body, affect your behaviour with others, and cause you to interpret

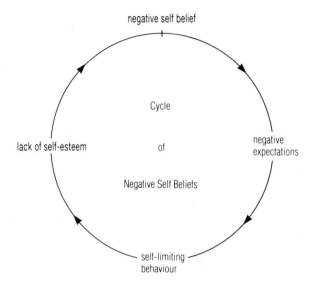

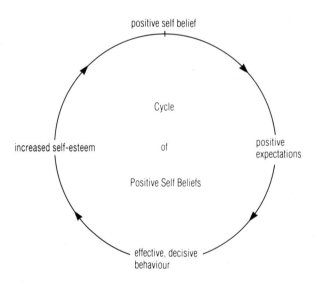

Figure 9   *Cycles of self belief and self-esteem*

events in the light of your beliefs. And so daily experience will seem to justify what you believe more and more.

We create our own personal reality by the magic of the 'Law of Attraction'. Basically this law states that we create what we think about. We live within an electromagnetic field and every time we think we charge the field around us with vibrations. Like attracts like and so negative thought patterns attract all forms of negativity. Similarly positive thought patterns attract all forms of positivity. We feel this effect at all levels of our being; we experience it spiritually, mentally, emotionally and physically.

If, as a small child, you were constantly being told that you were – stupid, lazy, thoughtless, nasty (or whatever) – it is highly probable that such beliefs are an integral part of your self image today.

Our feelings of self worth (or our lack of them) begin in the cradle. Unfortunately, although our parents probably loved us dearly, they may have not been able to express their feelings in a way which made it possible for us to understand how much we were loved.

5.

Your Self Concept

A poor self concept can be traced back to an early assimilation of negative ideas and attitudes about yourself. It is directly related to the extent to which you have been *invalidated*. We commonly use the word 'invalid' (noun) to describe a person who is *physically* disabled in some way. We can render something 'invalid' (adjective) and so take away its legitimacy and effectiveness. If I 'invalidate' you, I take away your effectiveness, legitimacy and power by making you *emotionally* disabled. This idea of *emotional disability* is very important.

Little Johnny is playing in the garden. He calls to mummy to tell her that he has something for her. He enters the house proudly carrying some mud 'cakes' he has made for her. He is covered in mud from head to toe. His mother takes one look and screams to him to get out of the house and to take that muck with him, he's never ever to bring mud into the house again. He should know never to come into the house without taking his boots off. Where has he been digging anyway? What, in the flower bed? 'You ought to know that you must never dig in the flower bed. Look how filthy you are. How am I ever going to get those clothes clean? Just leave that muck alone and come with me, I'll have to put you in the bath now. Oh you are so stupid and thoughtless, always causing me extra work. Never, never do that again.'

Johnny is confused, mummy is angry. There is a breakdown in communication. Both mother and child feel alone and unsupported. Johnny has been emotionally disabled by the person who probably has the greatest influence on him. Little Johnny had made mummy some lovely cakes and he felt so proud of himself. Mummy will be pleased with me, I will make her very happy – but mummy went mad with anger! This was not what he had expected. Johnny feels confused, worried, tense, unsure and probably many other frightening things. His good feelings about himself have been totally contradicted by his mother. Her reaction was not what he had expected. Who is he to believe? How can he trust his own feelings when they have been proved so 'wrong'? Is this what happens when he tries to be thoughtful? How can he ever trust his own decisions again?

Johnny has been invalidated by his mother. When we are invalidated we feel emotionally unsupported and we become confused. This can have a crippling effect on our development, and our self-esteem, especially if we are being constantly belittled.

When we validate someone we support their emotions. This doesn't mean that mummy invites little Johnny to make mud pies in the sitting room, but it does mean that she can ask him to change his future behaviour whilst still being able to accept his gift. She does not need to deny all his positive feelings in order to prevent him bringing mud into the house. How could she have dealt with this situation differently?

Johnny enters the door with his 'cakes'. Mummy is horrified but sees the pride in his face and knows that he is so excited that he has forgotten all the rules, like no mud in the house, no wearing boots in the house. Anyway the damage is already done – there are muddy footprints on the carpet. Is it worth making the child miserable and spoiling his delight? Is it *appropriate* to be angry here. What does it achieve? If you become confused and fearful as a child (or as an adult) you are unable to learn because you shut down all receptive channels in order to protect yourself.

Mummy can thank Johnny and he can feel proud of his creativity. He won't be afraid to make something for her again. She can take him outside and explain to him, without being angry, that although she loves the cakes she would rather that he didn't bring mud into the house and that he didn't dig up the flower bed. Perhaps he could dig over there where there are no flowers to spoil.

Johnny feels validated. Mummy agrees that he is a loving, creative, giving and thoughtful boy. He is happy and his positive self-belief cycle is in operation. He also 'heard' her telling him about the good place to dig and that she would prefer him not to bring mud inside. He is not confused and his self identity and his sense of self worth are intact. Mummy isn't left alone holding her anger. She has kept the lines of communication open between her and Johnny. She has supported his good feelings whilst also turning the event into a learning situation – this further validates their relationship. Mummy feels that she has dealt well with the situation and so feels good about herself; her positive self-belief cycle is also in operation. She has responded creatively to the situation and her self-esteem is high. *Validation makes everyone feel good!*

Our beliefs about ourselves are created by the interplay between that which we have learned to believe and the dynamics of the Law of Attraction. If our self-esteem is low then it follows that we have not been given sufficient validation during those very important early years. Perhaps you are already reaching into your past and remembering negative messages that you received from important people in your life: '. . . My mother was always telling me that I wasn't as clever as my sister . . . My big brother said I was a pathetic weakling every time I cried . . . Whenever I did badly at school my father said I was a lazy slob . . .' etc.

Perhaps you feel that you were well validated in your childhood and that consequently you have high self-esteem. If so, read no further. The sad fact is that everyone is still reading.

How do you feel about the people who so powerfully influenced your beliefs about yourself? '. . . Why did my mother do that to me? Didn't she love me? . . . Why did he (they) treat me like that? . . . How could they have done this to me? . . . I feel so angry with them it's all their fault'.

Is it indeed 'all their fault'? Remember that your parents were once children; they learned their beliefs the way that you learned yours. Were they emotionally supported?

In her book *Peoplemaking*, Virginia Satir refers to the family as the 'factory' where people are made. We, the adults, are the 'peoplemakers', and we are in the process of 'making' our children right now! Are we being emotionally supportive?

Whenever we invalidate someone we devalue them and ourselves, and everyone involved becomes low in self-esteem. When we are being emotionally supportive we are treating people with respect. This means that everyone feels free to express their feelings and to communicate their needs. Emotional support reinforces self-esteem and depends upon good communication.

6.

Communication

Our ability to create self-esteem relies on our communication skills. It is no good knowing what you want to happen if you are unable to make your meaning clear to others. When we look at the mechanics of face-to-face communication it is easy to see how misunderstandings and low self-esteem can arise during our interactions. Face-to-face communication works like this:

I meet you and my senses experience you. I can look at you, hear you, smell you and (maybe) touch you.

My brain then processes this information and makes certain perceptions which will be based largely on past (early childhood) learning experiences.

The messages from my brain will then affect my body – I will feel relaxed or uptight.

The same thing is happening to you. You too have sense experiences which are 'understood' by virtue of learned experience, values etc. I can know very little or even nothing about your sensory perceptions and how they affect your judgement; I can only guess. These guesses can become 'realities' to me, 'realities' which are totally unreal to you. Your 'realities' about me are probably similarly fantastic. How can we possibly have any meaningful communication?

Stuff and Nonsense

A good relationship is largely dependent on understanding another's meaning. It requires that we don't make guesses. It means that we *really* listen and that we have to ask questions if we don't understand what someone is saying. In order to meet these requirements we need to overcome our own limitations. This means being able to suspend our own limiting (negative) thought and behaviour patterns – what I call our personal *stuff*. This is the stuff of which our energy blocks are made. Our personal stuff prevents us from being open and trusting and able to take risks. It makes us fearful and closed and unable to understand what is being communicated. These limitations are truly only stuff and nonsense. Here is an example of personal stuff doing its dirty work.

A teacher is explaining to a pupil what she is setting for his homework. He feels threatened in some way – perhaps he is afraid of female authority figures, maybe her approach is very heavy – whatever the reason his panic buttons have been pressed. As she continues to explain, he stops hearing what she is saying and becomes bogged down in his own personal stuff. It goes something like this: '. . . what is she saying? . . . Is she going to tell me off? . . . Why can't I understand her? . . . It's because I'm stupid . . . I can't ask her to repeat it as she'll think I'm stupid. As the child has these thoughts he misses the instructions. If the teacher is also being affected by personal stuff then this will affect the clarity with which she is able to communicate her message. She may, for example, see her relationship with the boy only in power terms. If, for whatever reason, she is unable to understand that there is a serious lack of communication between her and the boy then joint confusion will escalate.

Teacher	Sees the child's blank face.
	Says – 'Repeat what I have just told you'.
Child	Feels afraid and can't reply.

Teacher	Thinks the child is insolent and disrespectful. Feels angry. Says – 'Why didn't you listen to me?'
Child	Becomes more fearful and closes down.
Teacher	Feels that the child has withdrawn. Feels invalidated and angry. 'Why doesn't he treat me with the respect I deserve?' Says 'Why are you so stupid?' Reinforces the child's belief in his own stupidity.
Child	Feels invalidated. Says nothing, has withdrawn.
Teacher	Feels that she must get an answer from him. Says – 'Did you understand the instructions I gave you?' The feeling underlying the statement is 'You'd better say yes'.
Child	Feels afraid to say no. Says 'Yes'. What he says bears no relation to what he thinks and feels.

Emotional Unavailability

There has been no meaningful communication here. *The lines of communication are closed* and both teacher and child feel invalidated. The teacher was unable to 'be there' emotionally – she denied the child any emotional support. In other words she was emotionally unavailable. Neither of them came away from the situation feeling good and the incident may well have far-reaching negative effects.

The teacher thinks the child is non-attentive / stupid / cheeky / lazy, for not understanding his homework. The child feels misunderstood, angry and stupid. He does not trust the teacher and so feels no respect for her. He feels invalidated or, in other words, emotionally disabled.

Emotional disability is a serious illness, all the more so because it is a very common complaint which usually goes undetected.

The child felt emotionally disabled and so was unable to say what he thought or felt. His sense of self worth was undermined, his self-esteem plummeted, and this created a panic situation. He became very anxious and probably experienced unpleasant physical symptoms such as sweating / sinking in the stomach / ringing in the ears / light headedness. He thinks 'I am worthless', and so invalidation by another turns into self invalidation.

At this point the boy shuts down – his sense of self worth has been threatened and so he withdraws in order to protect himself. He has also made himself emotionally unavailable and so there is no possibility of any real understanding between the two of them.

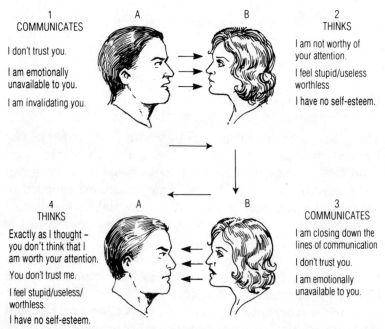

Figure 10   *Emotional Unavailability*

Emotional unavailability is an extremely infectious disease which has a very strange quality. We deliberately take on the illness so that we will be protected from the effects of it! If I become emotionally unavailable I cannot become emotionally disabled. In other words 'If I get you first you won't be able to get me'. Of course this doesn't work. Both parties become invalidated. There is no emotional winner and everybody is a loser, everybody loses self-esteem.

Figure 10 shows how easy it is to catch emotional unavailability. As a result of the interaction both A and B have no self-esteem.

Mixed Messages

When we close down for self protection we may become unable to communicate *or* we may say one thing whilst meaning something totally different. The teacher *says* 'Do you understand me?' but *thinks* 'You'd better say yes' and *feels* angry. These are mixed messages – they do not synchronize. She doesn't say what she means and so the child becomes confused. Similarly the child sends mixed messages. He says that he understands the instructions because he is too afraid to tell the truth. Lack of synchronicity of messages causes enormous problems in understanding; in fact it creates misunderstanding and confusion for everyone involved.

Fred is angry with Judith for being late. She is always a few minutes late when they arrange to meet. His words are pleasant but he speaks through clenched teeth and he is unable to make eye contact. Judith sees and feels the lack of synchronicity in Fred's messages. She tries to keep the lines of communication open by asking him what is the matter. He quickly denies that there is a problem. He finds, with relief, that he can act 'normally' now (that is, he can successfully disguise his real feelings) and for him an uncomfortable moment has passed – but has it? Judith is aware that Fred did not express his true feelings and she feels hurt. She decides to put on a 'brave face' so that Fred doesn't get angry again and for her an uncomfortable moment has passed – but has it?

We are particularly adept at covering our emotional tracks. We have been learning to tell emotional lies in order to 'keep up appearances' since childhood. But think of all the effort that was required to learn how to become emotionally unavailable. Was it worth it? Are you able to 'keep up a good front'? Do you need to 'protect' yourself in this way any more? Are you really protecting yourself?

We have looked at how successfully we can mix messages in order to confuse others. Even more sinister however is our ability to confuse ourselves.

Let's see what's happening to Fred and Judith. Well, they go out for the evening and Fred manages to store his anger somewhere deep inside him. In fact he completely forgets how angry he had felt towards Judith. Judith isn't quite so good at finding places to hide her feelings and she still feels hurt. As the evening progresses this hurt begins to turn into anger as she realizes that Fred has completely forgotten the incident and that she is still thinking about it. Judith eventually feels so angry that she resolves to 'get to the bottom of it'.

Judith	'What was the matter with you when we met tonight?'
Fred	'Nothing why?' He can't remember.
Judith	'Oh come off it. Do you think I'm stupid or something? You were really uptight.'
Fred	'Oh that, it was nothing.' He remembers.
Judith	'What do you mean? Of course it was something. Why won't you tell me?'
Fred	'Oh, why are you going on about it now, when we are out having a nice time? Why can't you just forget it? Come on let's just enjoy ourselves.'

Judith   'I can't enjoy myself, I keep thinking about it all the time. It's all right for you, you know what it's about.'

She shouts, 'Just tell me what it was about.'

She bursts into tears.

Fred   'Oh for God's sake shut up. Don't make a scene here. Trust you to get emotional.'

He is suddenly very angry and starts yelling at her for always being late. Why is she always late? Does she do it deliberately to wind him up? Why is she so stupid that she didn't even realize why he was so angry when they met? Judith is also very angry. Why doesn't he ever say what he means? Why does he always expect her to read his mind? She is always having to pretend that everything is OK.

Fred and Judith played equal parts in creating this scenario. They had an implicit agreement to collude. They both told lies for appearances' sake and there is no one to blame. Perhaps Fred looks like the villain of the piece. After all, Judith did ask him what was wrong at the beginning of the evening. However Judith soon joined the collusion when she 'put on her brave face'. Both tried to sit on their anger, which eventually became explosive. Fred entered a powerful danger zone. He was able to deny his feeling of anger, not only to Judith, but also to himself.

Every time we play the emotional unavailability game we strengthen the possibility that we become emotionally unavailable to ourselves. If this happens we lose touch with our own feelings and then, even if we want to communicate openly, we will be unable to do so because *we no longer know what we feel*. When we don't know how we feel we have lost our creative power, we are out of balance and we become victims with little or no self-esteem.

Let's take another look at the teacher / child scenario. Both were unable to 'be there' emotionally for each other.

Think of a recent situation where someone was unable to

'be there' for you. How did you feel? Stupid, worthless, angry, miserable, resentful, rejected, annoyed? You may have felt some or all of these things. One thing is sure – you didn't feel good about yourself.

Whenever we withdraw our 'beingness' during communication with someone we devalue them. We are sending unspoken messages which say, 'You don't deserve my attention . . . you are not worth listening to . . . I don't respect your feelings . . . you are worthless . . .'

7.

Validation

As we have learned ways to create misunderstanding, so we can learn techniques to facilitate understanding. We can learn to *open up the lines of communication*, and one way to do this is by validating each other. When we give each other emotional support in this way we become emotionally available to each other and self-esteem increases all round. Think of a recent situation where someone *was* able to 'be there' emotionally for you. How did you feel?

The teacher / child scenario could be different if the teacher is able emotionally to support (validate) the child. If the teacher is in touch with her own feelings, she may well recognize that the child is undergoing inner turmoil and doubt and so has been unable to hear what she has said. She does not interpret his silence as a personal attack.

Teacher	Says – 'Did you understand the instructions I gave you?' Feels that she wants to help the child to understand.
Child	Feels that the teacher is aware that he has a problem and that she will repeat the instructions if necessary. Feels able to 'risk' telling the truth. Says – 'I don't understand the instructions'.

The teacher genuinely wants good, open communication with the child and so is prepared to explain to him whatever is necessary. *The lines of communication are open.* She speaks and listens to him until she is sure that he knows what to do. The boy feels valued and the teacher feels valued by the child's response. The child's needs have been respected and so his feelings of self worth remain intact and he is not afraid to express what he truly thinks and feels.

Whenever we communicate and the lines are being kept open we are giving and receiving emotional support and we feel validated.

'*I deserve emotional support.*' How does it feel when you make this affirmation? Do you truly believe that you are worthy of validation? Self validation, validation *for* others and validation *by* others are intrinsically bound. If I am critical, denying, fearful and non-trusting of myself then I will project these feelings on to others who will reflect these feelings back to me. The Law of Attraction is at work.

- If we lack self respect then how can we feel respect for others? We don't know what respect feels like.
- If we are critical of self then how can we stop ourselves being critical of others? We only know how to be judgemental.
- If we are afraid of our feelings, and deny them, then how can we relate to the feelings of others? We don't know how to recognize them.

If we can feel self worth we can respect the worth of others. And so we return to self-esteem. The power to change your limiting beliefs depends upon the extent to which you love and value yourself.

As I cultivate my own nature all else follows.
Ralph Blum, *Book of Runes*

'*I love and value myself.*' Say this out loud to yourself. Say it again and again. Say it a hundred times. Sing it in the bath.

Say it to yourself at the bus stop, in the bus, in the car, in the dentist's chair, at the supermarket, say it everywhere!

Self validation is the key to change. If I love and value myself I am no longer afraid to keep the lines of communication open. I don't depend on your good opinion of me in order to feel good about myself. I am emotionally supporting myself and so I can 'be there' emotionally for you. You feel emotionally supported, which increases your feelings of self worth . . . and so the effects snowball.

Sounds too good to be true? Sounds too easy? Sounds just like a lot of words, and so it is until you *try* it. If you never read another word of this book it doesn't matter, so long as you give 'I love and value myself' a try. What have you got to lose apart from low self-esteem? Every time you say 'I love and value myself' you create magic in your life. This affirmation is a magic spell for change. Sounds impossible?

Try this. Look in a mirror and say 'I love and value myself'. How does it feel? Say it again. What does it feel like to look into your own eyes and say that you love and value yourself? It sounds such an easy thing to do. Is it easy for you? Some people find this a very difficult exercise. A common initial response is one of incredible embarrassment coupled with statements like, 'I can't say that, it sounds big-headed' or 'It sounds like I'm showing off'. Where did such ideas come from? Why were so many of us taught that it was 'not nice' to be supportive of ourselves, that somehow it was 'boastful'.

When I was nine and at primary school my mother made me some clothes for school sports day. I chose the pattern and the material, and I can see those clothes now in every small detail. The culottes were made from pink sailcloth and the sleeveless blouse was made from white cotton material with a pattern of tiny pink rosebuds which exactly matched the shorts. Even the bias binding around the neck and sleeve openings of the blouse matched the pink of the outfit. Those clothes were a work of art.

I felt absolutely wonderful when I wore them to school on sports day. I can still recall that very special feeling. We were told to get in line to go to the sports field and I can distinctly remember standing there watching Mrs Pilkinton approach. She wore a white dress with large blue flowers all over it and from that day until this I have hated Mrs Pilkinton. She walked up to me and said 'Well you are looking very smart today Lynda'. I felt overwhelmed by the wonderfulness of the world and blurted out, 'Yes aren't they lovely clothes'. Mrs Pilkinton looked down at me from her great height in a way which I have never forgotten. The Look held a mixture of disbelief, contempt, fury, hatred, scorn and lots of other things that I didn't recognize. If The Look was hard to describe its effects weren't. I started to shrink. Why couldn't I just disappear? I didn't feel special any more, in fact I felt like a worm. Time stood still and I was in absolute agony and total confusion. What had I done wrong? When I recall this moment I am happy to be able to say that despite my feelings of dejection I still retained an innate feeling of curiosity. What on earth was she going to say? I really couldn't imagine. Well, the anticipation was more exciting than the event. When she did speak it was an anticlimax. 'How dare you. Don't you know that you're not supposed to agree with people when they say nice things about you. You are just a boastful girl and you don't deserve nice clothes.' Oh so she thought that I had been showing off, that was what all the fuss was about. I wanted to shout out that I hadn't meant to be boastful and that I had only said what I had felt, but I didn't. I have no more memories of that day or of Mrs Pilkinton.

Had I been showing off or not? Regardless of the confusion of the moment I felt that I had been wrongly accused. I hadn't *meant* to boast, surely that was what was important. Oh the perception of youth! Time and time again I have returned to this memory which became a yardstick by which I measured future 'showingoffness'. This became especially useful when I discovered affirmations and started to say lots of nice supportive things to myself. Eventually I realized the importance of the understanding that I hadn't meant to boast. *Intention* is the key arbitrator and only I know my own intentions and only you know yours.

If you feel that you are boasting when you say 'I love and value myself', take a good look at your intentions. Why are you validating yourself? You are giving yourself emotional support and we have seen how important this is as an agent for change.

When we translated 'should' into 'could' we saw that it was sometimes possible to reach back into the past to unearth the sources of our limiting thought patterns. By taking full responsibility for our own actions and positively affirming that we 'could' do something if we really wanted to we can reveal the beliefs which restrict us. In this way positive affirmations *contradict* our deeply held negative affirmations. The magic of self validation by the use of affirmations lies in this contradiction.

Take a piece of paper and write 'I love and value myself'. Write this fifty times and whenever a negative thought enters your head just turn the page over and write it on the other side of the paper.

What was it like? Was it easy? Was it hard? The most interesting piece of the paper is the scribble on the back. What does yours look like? Have you written anything on the back? If not, the Law of Contradictions has not started to work yet and you need to do the task again. Did you do the exercise at all? If you didn't, you will never know if it works. If this statement truly holds the magic powers I am claiming for it, isn't it worth a try? What have you got to lose except your limiting beliefs?

We will look more closely at the use of affirmations and visualization in Chapter 15. Meanwhile, it is important to understand that, *all positive affirmations lead back to* 'I love and value myself'. If an affirmation isn't working for you it is because you are not loving and valuing yourself. You will always have an ongoing relationship with 'I love and value myself'. You will never have finished saying it. When you are low and you feel you can't be bothered with all these techniques and good advice, one little 'I love and value myself' can start the road to healing. Whenever you feel intimidated in any way use this magic spell. Say it to yourself over and over again. *You can never love and value yourself too much. You are totally lovable and valuable.*

Part 3

Feeling

Your pain is the breaking of the shell that encloses your understanding.

Kahlil Gibran, *The Prophet*

8.

On Icing a Cake, Being a Fraud and Open Secrets

Or, looking good, feeling bad and getting better.

Self-esteem and confidence are not the same thing. Self-esteem gives rise to confidence but we can appear confident without having self-esteem.

Eight-year-old Charlotte had the most beautiful birthday cake in the shape of a pair of ballet shoes. Although the cake looked just like a pair of pink silk ballet shoes it was of course only a cake. Charlotte couldn't bring herself to cut the cake and so we never tasted it; we never even knew what sort of cake it was.

Confidence can be seen as the icing on the cake. You are the cake and the decoration. Your icing totally covers your cake. If we spend a lot of time and effort on our 'icing', our decoration, we may not ever want to cut the cake and find out what it's made of. Cutting the icing (looking beneath our cover) may mean realizing that the way we look is not enough to sustain us and that can be quite frightening. If, however, we know what our cake is made of, our decoration becomes part of the cake. The cake remains accessible to us for re-examination when necessary. When we are building self-esteem we examine our ingredients – what they are,

how they blend together; we are conscious of our spiritual /
mental / emotional / physical 'parts'. We can decorate our
cake appropriately – the icing is just another ingredient.

Building confidence without self knowledge is a tricky
business. We don't know how much icing our cake can take
– we don't know how strong the cake is. What can it support? When there has been no attempt at conscious self
awareness but much confidence boosting the icing cracks as
it is unsupported. The cake begins to show through. There
are two options open to us here.

We can slap on a bit more icing and pretend that nothing
has happened – *looking good / feeling bad* – or we can take
a look at the cake – *looking bad / feeling bad / getting better*.

Our self image depends on the beliefs we hold about ourselves. In order to have a high self image (and so high self-
esteem) we need to be aware of the ingredients of our cake.

Our public image is the way that others see us. If our
cover is good it is possible to have a high public image
whilst having low self-esteem. If self image is low and public
image is high we have what I call 'the fraud principle': low
self image + high public image = the fraud principle.

Mark is a well-known local businessman with a high-
profile public image. Over the years he has been asked to sit
on this and that committee and to take a leading decision-
making role within the community. Initially Mark was
highly flattered by the prestige he began to enjoy within the
community and this boosted his self confidence. If he ever
felt uncertain he could always bluff his way out. Very slowly
Mark's icing began to crack and eventually he came for
counselling.

Mark had begun to have dreadful nightmares during
which he would find himself in humiliating situations. A
recurrent theme was one of turning over an examination
paper only to find that he could answer none of the questions, even though he had revised hard for the exam. He
also often dreamt that he was addressing a large audience

when suddenly he was unable to speak. In the dream he sees himself mouthing the words whilst his audience rolls around in the aisles laughing.

When I asked Mark what these dreams meant to him he said that he was always afraid that people would realize that he wasn't what he was 'cracked up to be'. He said that he was sure that one day 'they' would 'find him out' and that he was a 'fraud'.

'Being a fraud' is a very common theme in many people's lives. It implies that we have secrets about ourselves, secrets which we are afraid others might discover. We may have done something in the past which we don't want others to know about because it might affect their opinion of us. Our secret may be about some thought or feeling which we want to keep hidden. Our 'cover-up' job will involve us in more secret activities. Secrets are heavy burdens which grow increasingly heavy as we carry them and collect a support mechanism, i.e. more secrets to cover up the original.

Remember Fred and Judith. They had secret thoughts and emotions. They 'kept up a good front' to protect their hidden feelings.

Mark said that he felt the terror of his insecurities during his dreams and that he was now facing 'growing uncertainty' in his everyday life.

Insecurity lies within. Nothing can make us insecure. Security lies within. We can make ourselves secure.

If our self-esteem is high we can deal with situations in an honest and direct way. We need have no fear about expressing our feelings of anger, sadness, inability or whatever. These feelings do not make us worth less (worthless).

As Mark began to feel that it was acceptable for him to look at his own feelings, indeed that it was all right even to *have* these feelings, his life began to improve. Nowadays when the chairman of the committee doesn't have the answer he is able to say so. He is able to share the problem with the rest of the members. He doesn't need to pretend anything to protect his security. Mark doesn't feel a fraud any more. No one can 'find him out' because there is nothing to find out. His new relaxed and open approach has made him very popular and he is in great demand. Mark is presently working on learning to say no!

If our self-esteem is low we are sure to have secrets. These secrets are to do with things we don't like about ourselves. We often deny our experience of certain feelings – jealousy / anger / fear / grief are often suppressed. Are there any feelings which you find hard to claim? Why are we ashamed to admit to certain feelings? Why are they unacceptable to us?

9.

Feelings Matter

Great emphasis is placed on the necessity for us to take care of our physical needs but our emotional needs are less well catered for. In fact, we are taught from a very early age that feelings are best kept to ourselves. This denial of emotional expression stems from a fear of the power of feelings and a reluctance to express our needs. How can we keep control if we are overwhelmed by our emotions? If we show our emotional 'weaknesses' we will become vulnerable. Is this really true?

Did you hear any childhood messages like these? Put a smile on your face, stop being so miserable . . . Don't be afraid, just go and do it like the others . . . Boys don't cry . . . Boys aren't afraid . . . Be nice to your teacher – remember she's in charge . . . Don't get cross, people don't like it . . . No one will like you if you speak your mind . . . When you get angry you make me unhappy.

The ideas underlying these common messages are:

- Don't show your feelings.
- People don't like people who show their feelings.
- I am afraid of your feelings.
- I am afraid of my feelings.
- Deny your feelings and everyone will be happy.

Feelings are related to needs. If our needs are fulfilled then we feel all right; if they are not fulfilled then we don't feel all right. Whenever you deny your feelings you are pretending that you have no needs – you are having secrets and secrets are a heavy burden which you must carry alone.

If we become practised in the art of hiding our feelings from others (unexpressed feelings) we eventually become able to hide our feelings from ourselves (unacknowledged feelings). However, *hidden feelings don't go away* – they have to be hidden somewhere. We hide them inside ourselves and they cause us pain and misery at all levels of our being. We are not being honest with ourselves and so we feel ill at ease (dis-eased).

Sometimes we confuse the desire to think positively with the need to deny our feelings. This can happen very easily. Have your ever felt very sad about something and then rejected that feeling because 'It's best to look on the bright side of life'?

When we are thinking positively we are never denying our feelings. When you say 'I love and value myself' you are appreciating all 'parts' of yourself. You are loving yourself when you are feeling – happy, hurtful, guilty, horrible, fat, jealous, selfish, beautiful, thin, cowardly, isolated, peaceful, brave, unselfish, gorgeous and angry. You are giving yourself emotional support at all times and in all states.

Stages of Denial

Have you ever:

1. Been overwhelmed by a feeling?
2. Felt guilty or ashamed for having had such a feeling?
3. Denied that feeling?
4. Felt low self-esteem because of your denial?

Think for a moment and recall a time when you denied a feeling. How was your self-esteem at stage 2 of this process? Did you feel that you were a 'horrible' person for feeling so angry . . . envious . . . impatient . . . etc or did you feel stupid and out of control when you felt so sad . . . rejected . . . frightened . . . etc?

Liz suffers with all sorts of physical symptoms including lethargy, depression and headaches. After seeing Liz many times over the course of a few months her doctor suggested to her that she might improve her physical condition by seeking counselling support. At our first meeting Liz was very withdrawn and she said that she was feeling ill. Her posture was poor and she was unable to maintain eye contact for longer than a few seconds. Her body language indicated her very low self-esteem. Liz wasn't able to give me much background information at that meeting, but in a way this reluctance to talk told me quite a lot about her.

When we suppress our thoughts and feelings we close down the lines of communication. We 'keep ourselves to ourselves' and become isolated, unhappy and confused, and often we become ill. Remember that the condition of our physical, mental, emotional and spiritual 'parts' are inextricably bound – you can't affect one without affecting the others. Think about the ways that *your* feelings find physical expression. How does your body react to fear? Do you have a knot in your stomach, do you sweat, can you feel the adrenalin rushing through your veins?

Imagine a recent time when you were feeling afraid. Close your eyes and try to recreate the situation as clearly as possible. Feel your fear and check your bodily reactions.

How did your body respond? ....

Now recreate a situation when you were feeling very happy. How were your energy levels? Was there a spring in your step?

How did your body respond? ....

We all react differently so take some time here to think about the way your own body reacts to your own emotional states.

At our next meeting I encouraged Liz to talk to me about the members of her family. I was looking for clues in an effort to discover the feelings which Liz was hiding from me and also very possibly hiding from herself. As she talked about her sister, Michelle, Liz became more animated than I had ever seen her. She told me that Michelle was clever, successful, beautiful and happy and had everything going for her whilst she, Liz, had nothing. Eventually Liz was able to admit that she had always felt very jealous of her sister. She said that she hated herself for having such a wicked feeling. Liz had never admitted her jealousy before for fear of what people might think of her. She said that she wished that she hadn't told me because, 'It's much more comfortable to keep a lid on it. What good does it do to admit these things when it only makes me feel guilty and it doesn't change anything?'

We give our feelings power over us when we deny them. We become victims of our own emotional states. *There is no such thing as a negative feeling. Negativity lies in the denial of a feeling.*

Liz is jealous of Michelle. Liz thinks that it is unacceptable for her to feel jealous and so she tries to hide her feelings. Because Liz feels that it is 'not right' to feel jealous she feels guilty, and she also feels self hatred. By denying a *simple* feeling in order to protect ourselves we can create a *compound* of hidden feelings. This compound will eventually cause us pain. Let's see how Liz compounded her feelings by denial. She:

1. Feels jealous.
2. Hates herself / feels guilty.
3. Denies feeling jealous.
4. Feels even less self respect.
5. Has very low self-esteem.

Where has Liz put these feelings? She has hidden them inside herself and they are causing her pain – both emotional and physical. Compounded feelings create confusion at every level of our being. Her emotional pain can be shown as a self defeating spiral of confused feeling (Figure 11). Her physical pain is obvious. Remember how we were able to link certain feelings with specific physical responses? If, then, we suppress a feeling we also suppress the physicality (physical expression) of that feeling. *Feelings cannot go away if we continue to hold on to them. Physical symptoms cannot go away if we hold on to them.*

When we looked at our stuff (the emotional debris which creates our blocks) we were looking at all our unreleased compounded feelings and their related physical symptoms. If we can learn to let go of our feelings we can stop creating the stuff which creates blocks to our freely flowing energy. We can live a balanced life and enjoy high self-esteem.

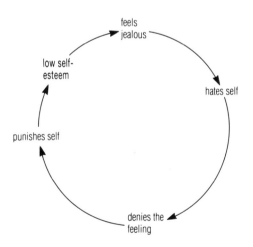

Figure 11   *How feelings are compounded when you deny them*

Head and Heart

Sit very still, close your eyes and ask yourself, 'How do I feel at the moment?' Happy . . . sad . . . miserable . . . hopeful . . . angry . . . excited . . . fearful . . . serious . . . loving . . . hopeless . . . frightened . . . confident? Do you know how you feel? Can you tell the difference between your thoughts and your feelings? Sometimes it is hard to know what we are feeling because we have become out of touch with our emotions. We are listening to our head and not our heart.

If we want to clear our emotional debris we need to *let go* rather than to deny our feelings. We cannot let go of a feeling until we know what that feeling is. We need to acknowledge a feeling before we can let it go. Susie Orbach has used the phrase, 'emotional illiteracy' to describe our inability to acknowledge our true feelings and to act upon them and so to let them go. Ms Orbach suggests that:

> The institutions which shape our experience from the cradle to the grave unwittingly brutalise the personal. Our emotional needs get exploited rather than addressed. We reward ourselves for achievement, for managing everything, for not collapsing and most fundamentally for not needing.
> S. Orbach – Weekend Guardian, *Feeling Our Way Through*
> Feb. 23/24 1991

When we were very young we were all extremely good at recognizing our needs and expressing our feelings. We need to re-learn these arts. It is not so difficult, it just takes a bit of practice.

Give yourself some *feeling checks* throughout the day. This means that whenever you remember, stop for a moment and ask yourself, 'What am I feeling now?' As you practise this technique you will become more and more aware of your feelings. You are learning to listen with your heart.

When I asked Liz to practise getting in touch with her feelings she was very reluctant. She said that she couldn't bear the pain of her feelings. Shakti Gawain suggests that:

. . . it is our resistance to a feeling that causes us pain. If, because we are afraid of a certain feeling, we suppress it we will experience emotional pain. If we allow ourselves to feel it and accept it fully, it becomes an intense sensation, though not a painful one.

This also applies in exactly the same way at the physical level. Imagine yourself in the dentist's chair. You are going to have an injection to freeze your gum. You see the dentist coming towards you with the needle . . . and then what do you do? Well I automatically become rigid. Every part of me becomes tense as I prepare for the pain, and then I remember that if I relax and take some deep breaths my experience of the injection will be different. There, I did it. I just remembered to relax in time. That wasn't so bad. I'm feeling pretty pleased with myself; yes I'm managing this pain control pretty well and then . . . *gasp* . . . that hurt! He's drilling away and in the very short time that I spent congratulating myself I became rigid again. Well I spend many happy times in the dentist's chair remembering not to resist and then forgetting again immediately. Old habits die hard!

If we deny our feelings 'in case they hurt' we will get stuck. Our energy becomes blocked and things start going wrong as we begin a negative downward spiral.

Liz is stuck in her jealousy and the other assorted feelings which she has collected – guilt / self hatred / anger etc. None of these feelings makes her feel good. In fact she feels lousy. Why is she sticking in this pile of emotional debris? She says it is because she can't bear the 'pain' of her emotions. I asked her if this pain which she expects could make her feel any worse than she feels right now. Liz said that she couldn't sink any lower so she might as well try a new approach.

10.

To Suppress or Express?

Imagine that you are surrounded by beautiful coloured bubbles. All the bubbles are different in size and colour and they are floating around, gently bumping in to each other and then floating off in another direction. These bubbles represent the whole range of the emotional responses which you have experienced. They are many and varied. They are colourful and they are unique and they are an expression of your individuality. They are fascinating – you are fascinating!

When Liz first experienced her jealousy of her sister she created a bubble of feeling which surrounded her. Liz became trapped in this bubble because she refused to see that it was there. This first 'jealousy bubble' was her initial simple feeling. Other bubbles of anger / self hate / guilt and so on were attracted to this bubble. The bubble enlarged and became a compound of many feelings. How can Liz escape?

If *suppression* causes the problem then *expression* can negate it. Suppressed feelings are the result of denial and expressed feelings are the result of acceptance. When we feel something and thus create the bubble of that feeling around us we can only walk out of that particular bubble by *moving through it*. This requires that we experience the *whole* bubble. We have to feel the feeling right through, and the trick is to keep moving. Move along with the feeling, go where it takes you. The experience may be intense but it will not cause you pain. Remember that *pain lies in resistance.*

Liz denied her jealousy and became trapped in a bubble of confused feelings. It took her many years of mental and physical ill health before she was ready to separate out her compounded feelings to discover her jealousy. Liz and I used the 'letting go process' (below) to enable her to release her jealousy. At first Liz said that she found it 'impossible' to forgive herself or her sister. However eventually, after a few weeks of work, both with me and alone at home, a magic day arrived when Liz found forgiveness in her heart. She forgave her sister and forgave herself, and from that moment the letting go became easier. (Forgiveness is discussed further in Chapter 12). By letting go of her jealousy, Liz has let go of the emotional ties which bound her to Michelle. Liz had always lived in her sister's shadow and now she feels ready to live her own life.

Stages of Letting Go

1. You have been overwhelmed by a feeling.
2. And then you *accept* that you have this feeling.
3. And so you move along with the feeling and experience all parts of it.
4. And then you are able to *let go* of the feeling.
5. Emerging from the process with your self-esteem intact.

This process is much simpler than it sounds. The key to success in the letting go process is the ability to *accept* your feelings whatever they might be. There is no point in disowning the 'bits' of ourselves which we don't like; we can't change these 'bits' until we accept them.

When we looked at the stages of denial I asked you to

remember a time when you denied a feeling. Can you now think of a feeling which you are in the process of denying? This would be a recent feeling which you find unacceptable. Are you ready to let go of this feeling? If so, take a piece of paper and a pencil and complete the following statements in as much detail as is necessary. You will probably need some privacy for this task.

The Letting Go Process

I .... (name) am denying that I feel ....
I .... am denying that I feel .... because ....
....
I .... am ready to accept that I feel ....
I .... accept that I feel ....
I .... love and value all my experiences.
I .... love and value all of my feelings.
I .... give myself permission to feel ....

You are now allowing yourself to experience the denied feeling. You may be experiencing all sorts of associated feelings. Are you? If so, acknowledge these feelings – say them – write them down – find a way to express all that you are feeling at the moment. Do you feel guilty or angry with yourself? If so take up your pencil again and write:

I .... forgive myself.

Do you feel angry with anyone else? If so write:

I .... forgive you .... (name of person).

All this forgiveness may very well make you feel more anger. Don't be afraid of the intensity of your feelings. *Your feelings cannot hurt you.* The deeper the intensity of your feelings, the more you are letting go. If you do feel afraid of the depth of your feelings at any time during this exercise, just acknowledge and express your fear. You could write:

I .... am frightened of my feelings.

Whenever you express your fear you will feel less frightened.
Whenever you express your anger you will feel less angry.
Whenever you express your guilt you will feel less guilty.

Writing your feelings is one way to express them. Other ways of private expression include speaking your written statements out loud. A very powerful way is to speak out loud into a mirror. Sounds a bit crazy? Try it. Try anything which will help you. If you are angry try pillow bashing. If you are sad let yourself cry.

There may come a time when you feel like sharing your feelings. Talking to someone whom you trust may help. You could use the letting go exercise and read your statements to the other person. You may feel the need for some professional counselling support.

Choose the method(s) which suit you and when you need a different approach change your method(s) accordingly. Be flexible and allow yourself to experiment. The importance doesn't lie in the method, it lies in the result. If a particular technique works for you, then use it. As you move from denial into acceptance the effect will be felt in all areas of your life.

Human beings can never feel self respect if they live in denial. If we don't know what self respect feels like, how do we know how to feel respect for others? If you can accept your feelings you will be able to feel self respect (and consequently self-esteem). You will recognize my intrinsic self worth and so our communication with each other will be open and mutually supporting.

Denial of feelings has far-reaching consequences. If I am unable to respect my needs I can't respect the needs of others and neither can I respect the needs of our ecological system. Is this why there is such a proliferation of self abuse,

abuse of others and abuse of the earth's resources? Does planetary transformation depend upon self transformation? If you respect yourself you will be able to respect *all* the natural world. People who are high in self-esteem treat our planet with the care and sensitivity which it deserves.

11.

It's OK to be Angry

You shouldn't be angry because it hurts people . . . If I show that I am angry I lose control . . . If you are angry you can never be at peace . . . When I feel angry I really let rip; it gets the steam out of me . . . It never does me any good to be angry because I always feel guilty afterwards . . . If I get angry my wife cries, so I try not to show it . . . If my children see me being angry they will grow up to be angry people . . . Being angry is an immature response. Children lose their tempers quickly, we should learn to control our tempers as we get older . . . People don't like you if you get angry . . . If someone shows their anger I get frightened. I feel that if I ever expressed my anger I might get physically violent . . . I always try to calm everything down whenever anyone starts to get angry . . . My father used to get angry and hit me. I never get angry and hit my children – I just ignore them when they upset me . . . Men shouldn't get angry with women . . . When my wife gets angry I always put it down to women's troubles . . . I feel good when I'm expressing my anger – it's like opening a release valve, but afterwards I feel terribly depressed . . . I have felt and expressed a lot of anger in my life but it hasn't helped me.

I asked a lot of people what they felt about anger. These

were some of the responses. Do you relate to any of these replies? If so, which ones?

....

My friend Maureen described a familiar scenario. She said that she was feeling terrible because she had gone 'absolutely crazy' that morning at breakfast time. One of her children had spilled a drop of milk on the table and Maureen went absolutely berserk. The whole family watched in astonished silence as she jumped about performing a war dance in her nightie and slippers. After a noisy finale she collapsed into tears on the sofa. The offending child came and said sorry for spilling the milk and asked his mum if she was all right. Maureen had shouted back, 'All right? Does it look as though I'm all right? Does it sound as if I'm all right?' She said that by then she hadn't the energy for another explosion and anyway she was beginning to feel guilty. She also felt rather foolish when her five-year-old looked admiringly at her and said 'Mum you were brilliant' whilst the others stifled their giggles. Eventually Maureen found her sense of humour and everyone tried especially hard to make a quiet and hasty exit to school. Maureen knew that the spilt milk was not the important issue. She said that, 'If it had been spilled yesterday I possibly wouldn't even have noticed. (It probably was and I didn't.)' Hence Maureen's family was bemused as well as amused by her behaviour.

Often we appear to become angry for the most trivial of reasons. Can you remember a time when you became explosively angry over a seemingly unimportant incident? How did you feel after your outburst? After 'letting rip' in this way it is easy to then feel both guilty and foolish. Have you experienced this sequence of feelings? You explode with anger . . . and then . . . you feel guilty and foolish . . . and then . . . you feel angry with yourself . . . and by then . . . you have totally invalidated yourself.

- We experience confused feelings if we haven't expressed the real reason for our anger, and
- We feel misunderstood because nobody understands why we are so angry, but
- They can't understand because we haven't told them.

What is happening here? Do you remember the image of emotional bubbles? Well let's take the image of a bubble of anger and change it into a volcano of anger. Here (Figure 12) is someone who became angry, denied his anger and became trapped in a volcano. He becomes angry about something else and the heat mounts in the volcano. Every time this person is angry and denies it, the volcano gets hotter ... until *explosion*. The most trivial of incidents often ignites all the rest. The pressure is too great to bear. It all becomes too much.

Here (Figure 13) is Maureen in her volcano and the final layer (anger over spilt milk) has erupted. There's not much room left in her volcano to store any more anger. In fact

Figure 12   *The emotional volcano*

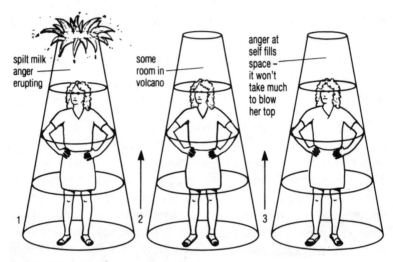

Figure 13   *Maureen's volcano*

Maureen's so angry with herself for losing control and looking foolish this morning that she`s fast filling up her volcano
with anger at self. There's very little room left – one tiny
anger-making incident and her volcano will erupt again!

This is a very stressful way to live. Again the problem lies
with denial. People often deny their anger because they know
that they are sitting in a minefield of unexploded emotion
and they are afraid that they will be lost in the explosion.

Each time we deny our anger we lose touch with ourselves
a bit more. When we can accept our anger we start to find
ourselves again. When the much-feared 'explosion' occurs
we will reclaim our self-esteem. We won't lose ourselves –
we will find ourselves. Shakti Gawain says:

> When we suppress our true power and allow other people to
> have undue power over us, we become angry. Usually we sup-
> press this anger and go numb. As we start to get back in
> touch with our power, the first thing we feel is the stored-up
> anger. So for many people who are growing more conscious,
> it's a very positive sign when they begin to get in touch with
> their anger. It means they are reclaiming their power.

The next time your volcano erupts, recognize your chance to really let go of some stored anger. Don't stop when you feel guilty or foolish. Remember this can be a positive experience for you. Don't stop the flow of feeling by trying to work out why you are angry. Shakti Gawain also uses the analogy of the volcano and says:

> ... just allow yourself to feel the anger and recognise that it is your power. Visualise a volcano going off inside of you and filling you with power and energy.

As your personal volcano erupts and you begin to let go of your stored-up anger you may need to express your feelings in a physical way. Give yourself permission to show this anger. Create a safe place where you can be free to shout, cry, thump pillows, jump around and do whatever you feel like. Claim your angry feelings as your own. They belong to you and no one else. So take responsibility for the ways in which you express your anger.

At certain times you may need to talk to someone with whom you feel safe. Start emptying that volcano and taking charge of your own life. As you begin to accept your anger you will find it much easier to express anger as you feel it. This is very important because it means that you will no longer be storing anger. We will be discussing this later when we look at assertion techniques. Meanwhile, enjoy reclaiming your power and increasing your self-esteem. Letting go of your anger will be an intense experience but it won't be painful . . . pain lies only in denial. Shakti Gawain says:

> An important key in transforming anger into an acceptance of your power is learning to assert yourself. Learn to ask for what you want and do what you want to do without being unduly influenced by other people. When you stop giving your power away to other people you won't feel angry any more.

Our social conditioning ensures that, for most of us, anger is one of the most difficult feelings to claim. Whenever we deny our feelings we are denying our needs and so we victimize ourselves. When you stop giving away your power you are no longer a victim, you are balancing yourself at the emotional level. As soon as we start to balance our energies we begin to take control of our destiny by learning how to respond creatively. When we are operating from a state of creative consciousness we are high in self-esteem.

12.

The Magic of Forgiveness

A Poison Tree

I was angry with my friend
I told my wrath, my wrath did end.
I was angry with my foe:
I told it not, my wrath did grow.

And I watered it with fears,
Night and morning with my tears:
And I sunned it with smiles,
And with soft deceitful wiles.

And it grew both day and night,
Till it bore an apple bright.
And my foe beheld it shine,
And he knew that it was mine.

And into my garden stole,
When the night had veild the pole;
In the morning glad I see
My foe outstretched upon the tree.

William Blake

Undo Your Past
In the Present
and Liberate Your Future
by Letting Go

As we contradict our old thought patterns with positive affirmations we are able, eventually, to let go of our limiting beliefs. Our future need no longer be ruled by our past. We can give ourselves the freedom to live in the here and now, to make spontaneous decisions and to be truly alive, unfettered by the doubts and insecurities which we have developed in our childhood.

During this process of contradiction we will inevitably uncover the identity of some (or all) of the people who taught us our limiting beliefs. These discoveries may be very painful experiences. (Mrs Pilkinton, wherever you are out there, I forgive you.) How could my mother have done that to me? . . . Why did my own father make me feel so worthless? . . . They can't have really loved me if they couldn't give me the emotional support I needed . . . and so on.

Have you unearthed a source of any of your limiting beliefs? If so, how do you feel about the person in question? Do you feel angry / sad / let down / shocked / unloved / accusing? All these are common emotional reactions. Perhaps you have other feelings, if so make a note of them. These feelings are important and need to be expressed. However there is no point in discovering the source of a limiting belief if we become stuck in accusation / anger and so on. Blake's 'Poison Tree' shows how the repression of anger can breed hatred so that one person can rejoice in the downfall of another.

We find it hard to forgive when our resentment has not been released. Unexpressed anger curdles and sours within us and so we can become bitter (and ill). Whenever we suppress our feelings we also suppress the physicality (physical expression) of those feelings. In this way our thought patterns can create illness in our bodies – our mind, body, spirit and emotions are so closely interrelated.

If I hold on to angry feelings about you I form a permanent relationship with you – I am bound to you in hatred. We are locked together with the handcuffs of unforgiveness. *The state of unforgiveness lowers self-esteem.* How can I love and value myself if I am thinking poisonous thoughts?

Forgiving doesn't mean saying that you are overlooking whatever happened that made you so angry. In fact it means the opposite. When we forgive we 'let go' of the ties that bind us to another in hatred. We let go of the need to be connected to that person any more. We are free to be ourselves without being hindered by reactive responses. To achieve this release we need to look carefully at what hurt us and we need to express this in some appropriate way (see Chapters 10 and 11).

Julia is a colleague of mine who is working hard on her own personal growth. She told me that she felt that she had a 'great lump of anger' within her and that she didn't know where to put it. Have you ever had this feeling?

Things are not as bleak as they seem. You can dissolve your own anger.

If my anger is of recent origin (that is to say it hasn't been stewing away for some time) there are a number of ways I can release it. If the 'lump' is small then it may be enough for me to shout a bit and bang a few pillows around (all in the privacy of my own home of course). This treatment is one of my favourites (although the rest of my family aren't so keen).

It may only be necessary to talk to someone about my feelings – it is possible to clear the air in this way so long as the 'lump' is small and only recently acquired.

If you feel better after using these methods then they have worked. The feeling of 'letting go' is one of lightness and release – you will know when you have let go of your anger.

Perhaps these methods weren't enough. You still feel angry. What can you do? This was how Julia felt when she came to see me.

The vital question to ask yourself here is, 'Where is this anger directed?' For a lump of anger to achieve some size we need a target to blame.

Julia said that she was angry with her brother who 'is a waster and always has been. He lives at home and my mother is still cooking his meals and ironing his shirts and he's thirty-four. Every time I go to mum's I feel really furious with him.' I asked her if she had told her brother what she had felt. 'Oh yes I told him all right. I'm always telling him how cross I am with him for taking advantage of mum. He doesn't take any notice of me. He just laughs. I feel so frustrated. Once he even said that mum would be lost without him. How conceited!'

I asked Julia how she thought her mother felt about this situation.

'Well you know mum has always been soft with Michael. He is the youngest and she's always done everything for him. He's so selfish, doesn't he realize that he's ruining my mum's life? We asked her to come on holiday with us last year but she couldn't because she had to be here to cook his meals. Honestly, after dad died I thought she'd get out and about a bit. After nursing dad for so long you'd think she deserved a rest. I asked her to come and stay with us after the funeral but she said she couldn't because "Mikey" needed her at home. She's always called him "Mikey". For God's sake, he's a grown man!'

Julia was beginning to sound angry now. Who is the real target here? I asked her to tell me about her childhood relationship with Michael, had she disliked him then? 'Oh no he was a sweetie. I used to like looking after him. You know, taking him to the park and things like that.'

'Did your mother ask you to look after him?'

'Oh no, she hated it. She used to want him to stay at

home and keep her company. She didn't like it when Mikey said he wanted to play with me. She used to let me go out but he wasn't often allowed. He used to get very upset and I felt really angry with her. Why did she do that?'

Julia was upset. I asked her how it felt to leave Mikey at home when she was allowed to go out. 'I hated it. I never used to enjoy myself, I kept wondering what they were doing at home, I felt so left out.' (Crying.) 'Why didn't she ever want me to stay at home with her? It wasn't even as if Mikey enjoyed staying with her – he hated it. It was me who wanted to stay with her, but she never wanted me.' (More crying.) 'I hate her for never wanting me! Oh what have I said?' Stunned silence for a couple of minutes.

'Oh God I feel so awful. You can't say that you hate your own mother can you? I feel so guilty. I've never said anything like that about her before. Look, I don't really mean that I hate her, I love her really. I wouldn't be so upset if I didn't care about her would I?' Julia floundered in a sea of emotions – guilt / denial / hatred / love / need – and possibly others. In the midst of her emotional turmoil she said, 'What am I feeling? I don't know what I am feeling any more.'

At this point I asked Julia if she would like to be free of this emotional web. She said she would and so I asked her to 'let go' of this emotional entanglement by forgiving her mother.

There is one very effective and thorough way to let go of the emotional ties which bind us to another person. I call this method 'The Forgiveness System'. I know of no other technique in personal growth therapy which has the power of this method.

What does it do? How does it work? Will it work for me?

Every time you use this technique you will improve the quality of your life. Isn't it worth a try? You have nothing to lose except a host of frightening emotions.

The Forgiveness System

Choose someone whom you would like to forgive. There will be plenty of people to choose from. We have tied ourselves to many people with our angry thoughts. Take a large piece of paper and write on the first line:

I .... (name) forgive you .... (name)

Then do it again. Whenever you feel or think anything in particular as you are writing, turn the page over and write it down. Be aware of whatever happens to you as you are doing your forgiveness. When you forgive someone in this way you are making a positive affirmation about your intention towards that person. The intention is that you are both going to be released from the bondage of unforgiveness. Naturally this affirmation will bring up all the negative contradictory beliefs you have held about this person. It may take a while before you experience any inner reaction to your forgiveness. Whatever does or doesn't appear to be happening, just keep on forgiving.

Write the affirmation thirty-five times every day for ten days. Don't give up and don't keep looking for results. Just keep writing the affirmation and keep writing the responses.

How do you feel after ten days of forgiveness? What feelings have you experienced? What have you discovered about yourself?

Julia had initially felt that her 'lump' of anger was related to her brother's behaviour. He was to blame. As she began to express her emotions it became clear that the relationship between her anger and its 'cause' was less direct than she had believed. By forgiving her mother, Julia discovered some very important things about herself. She was surprised to discover that her own feelings of guilt figured largely in her responses. When we offer forgiveness we can let go of our own guilt. This feels *fantastic* – try it and see!

Julia eventually reached a point of great revelation. She rang me excitedly one day. 'I've found out something incredible. I started by blaming Mikey and discovered that it wasn't his fault, and then I blamed mum and then I blamed me for being so horrible. Then I didn't know what to do so I forgave myself. I forgave myself for ten days and I discovered that it wasn't my fault either. We are all trying our best aren't we? It's just that we don't always know what the best is. I feel that I can stop blaming and start living. I feel like I'm in a powerful place.'

Forgiveness is a great discloser of the truth. If you keep forgiving, all will eventually be revealed – it becomes impossible to deceive yourself. You will become a person who is free to love and value yourself and you will be high in self-esteem. This is truly a 'powerful place' to be.

Forgiveness is a type of energy exchange which brings more to both giver and receiver. It reverses the physical laws. If A gives something to B then logically A hasn't got it any more. This is a physical law of the universe. But if A can release B by forgiveness then both A and B receive a true gift.

The magic of forgiveness cannot be explained: it can only be experienced. *Go ahead and experience it.*

Part 4

Acting

Whatever you can do or dream you can, begin it. Boldness has genius, power and magic in it. Begin it now.

Goethe

Part 4a

Acting

13.

Are You a Victim?

Our beliefs lie at the root of all our behaviour. If we are high in self-esteem we believe in ourselves, and our behaviour will support our positive self concept. If we are low in self-esteem, this will be demonstrated in our behaviour, which will reinforce our negative self concept. Figure 14 shows how our self concept affects the way we relate to the outside world. Our beliefs about self, others and the world are the result of our conditioning – we become set to expect and assume certain things. The ways in which we have externalized these beliefs have similarly become habitual, and to change our ways often involves overcoming a lifetime of conditioning.

If we change our beliefs a change in our actions will eventually follow. However this may take some time. Similarly, if we try to change our behaviour patterns we will question the validity of our set of beliefs – this also may be a lengthy procedure.

We have looked at the use of affirmations and how they can change habitual thought patterns. By working on our personal growth at all 'levels' of our being we greatly enhance the effect. All the approaches (connecting, understanding, feeling and acting) are designed to challenge any long-held beliefs, assumptions and expectations which limit

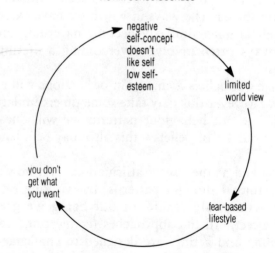

Figure 14 *The two cycles of consciousness*

us in any way. In this part of the book we will be looking at the ways in which we can change habitual behaviour patterns which are no longer working for us.

Figure 14 illustrates two different lifestyles. One operates from a state of creative consciousness and the other from a state of victim consciousness. Creative consciousness is a state of mind which allows us to take control of our lives. We are high in self-esteem and we can take responsibility for what happens to us. Victim consciousness is a state of mind which permits us to hand over all responsibility to someone else. We are low in self-esteem and we can blame 'them' for doing things to us and thus we are not accountable for whatever happens in our lives.

Why would I want to hand over the responsibility for myself to someone else? In other words what's 'in it' for me to become a victim? Some likely answers include:

- I'm afraid to stand up for myself.
- My feelings of self-esteem are low.
- My own self image depends on people liking me.
- I don't know how to stand up for myself.

Can you think of any other reasons?

In this context, I am by definition a victim, if I have lost control over my own life because I cannot take responsibility for myself. If you feel that your life isn't working for you in some way then you are allowing yourself to be victimized.

All our decision making and action taking is motivated by our beliefs about ourself and our world. Being a victim requires that we think that we are not worthy of the best and so we deserve to be manipulated by others.

Are there any areas in your life where you feel that you are being victimized? If so can you specify these areas? Do you know who is victimizing you and why?

Victim Questionnaire

Discover your victim status by answering yes or no to the following questions.

At Home

1. Is it difficult for you to say 'no' to family members?
2. Do you ever feel that your children take you for granted?
3. Do you feel appreciated by your partner and/or children?
4. Are you able to express your feelings to the members of your family?

At Work

1. Do you enjoy your job?
2. Do you always work late when asked, even if you don't want to?
3. Are you able to express your opinions if you disagree with 'superiors' at work?

Out in the World

1. You have a pair of shoes which split a month after you bought them.
   (a) Would you take them back?
   (b) If 'yes' would you feel anxious when taking them back?
   (c) If the shopkeeper says that the shoes have suffered fair wear and tear do you give up and go home?

(d) If you pursue the matter do you become angry or anxious?

2. Do you just pay the dentist's / solicitor's / accountant's bill even if you think you have been overcharged?

3. A market researcher stops you in the street in your lunch hour. Do you:
   (a) Just answer the questions even though you don't want to?
   (b) Say that you are not interested in answering the questions?
   (c) Say that you are not interested and feel guilty?
   (d) Say that you are not interested and proceed to justify yourself by explaining why you haven't the time to answer the questions?

4. Is it difficult to call your dentist / doctor / solicitor / accountant / child's headteacher etc by his / her first name?

5. You dislike the table which you have been given in the restaurant. Do you speak up?

Being Yourself

1. You are introduced to a group of strangers. Do you feel intimidated?

2. Do you ever ask permission to be allowed to speak or act in some way?

3. You have worked hard to achieve something and you have received a compliment. Do you say:
   (a) Thank you?
   (b) Oh it wasn't anything?

4. Do you often find yourself apologizing for your behaviour?

How did you fare on the victim test? Were you surprised by any of your replies? Would you like to be able to change any of your responses? If so, look at the situations in which you feel victimized. Why do you think that you are vulnerable in these particular areas?

We teach people the way we expect them to treat us, and we do this by the messages which we communicate. Our ability to negotiate our personal rights is therefore directly linked with our ability to communicate our wishes clearly to other people.

The following exercise will help you to see if you are able to communicate your needs adequately.

Self Profile Indicator

Answer the following questions, using these options:
- Untrue
- Sometimes true
- Often true
- True

1. I like to show my feelings.
2. I am frightened of meeting new people.
3. I don't like to get too close to anyone.
4. I can usually approach my life in a positive way.
5. I don't always know my true feelings.
6. I am able to express my ideas easily.
7. I worry about other people's opinion of me.
8. I am a good listener.
9. I usually put others' needs before my own.
10. I know how to trust my intuition.
11. I am self critical – I put myself down.
12. I enjoy making new friends.

13. I find it difficult to say 'no'.
14. I feel confident when starting something new.
15. I enjoy my own company.

Look at your answers. Choose the two qualities which you most admire about yourself. Write them down.

....

....

In what ways do you think that these attributes help you to communicate your needs effectively? Write these down.

....

....

Are there any qualities which you would like to change? If so what are they?

....

....

How do you think that these qualities affect your ability to communicate clearly?

....

....

Take a blank sheet of paper and 'brainstorm' for any ideas which may help you to change those qualities which you feel are limiting. Give yourself five minutes in which to write down any and every idea which comes to you. Put everything down; don't stop to evaluate your ideas. This technique is very effective for reaching into parts of the brain which other methods cannot reach.

Take a look at your list. Underlying any of your ideas to facilitate change will be the need to take risks. If you want to change, to act differently, you take a plunge into the unknown. You may feel too afraid to take a risk. Look at your ideas again. Are there any that you dare to try?

Anne is fifty years old. She is a mother of four children and a grandmother of five. She worked in a factory until she was made redundant two years ago and her husband died four years ago. A friend had brought her to see me because Anne was too frightened to come alone. In fact Anne was 'too frightened' to do almost anything. Anne agreed to do the self profile indicator and she was unable to find a single quality that she could admire about herself. She felt that she didn't possess any communication skills. Then she added that, 'Perhaps I am a good listener but then only because I'm too afraid to say anything.' She didn't know which qualities she would like to change. She said, 'I don't know who I am. I've never felt able to be "really me". I can't remember ever being not terrified in my life. Oh except one time when I was about seven years old.

'I used to take a packed lunch to school and a girl in my class used to take my biscuits or cake or whatever my mother used to give me. On the day I started school this girl called Susan looked in my lunch box and took out my cake. Every morning after that she would say "Hand it over then Anne" and I gave her whatever treat mum had put in. I never ever questioned her right to eat part of my lunch. I had been "handing over" for about two years when one day mum said that she wanted me to bring my biscuit wrappers home because she was collecting the tokens for something. I was horrified. What was I going to do? I remember trying to think of a way to keep Susan and mum happy. The only thing I could think of was to ask Susan to give me the wrapper back when she had finished. When I asked her I remember that my knees were shaking and she just laughed at me. Then I just saw red and swung my fist at her face. I made her nose bleed and I was put in detention for bad behaviour. That was the only detention I ever had. I was frightened that the teachers wouldn't like me any more and I was terrified that my mum would find out what I had done – but she never did. Susan never asked for anything from me again.

'It all seems so ridiculous now but I didn't learn anything from that incident. I only hit Susan because I completely lost my temper. I can't remember any other time in my life when I allowed myself to feel that angry again. I learned not to show my feelings and in the end I didn't even know what they were.

'I married the first man who asked me because I was so grateful that someone had asked. He took over my whole life and decided everything for me and now he's dead. I'd always gone along with his ideas and so I haven't got any of my own. I'm afraid to step out of my own door. Some new people have moved in next door and I'm so afraid of meeting them that I hang my washing out at night in the dark.'

How had Anne managed to come and tell me these things about herself if she was so frightened? It must have taken a lot of courage for her to come. Yes, she agreed, but only her desperation had brought her here.

We talked a bit about courage and what it takes to be prepared to take risks. Anne said, 'Well anything is better than feeling the way I do now.' Sometimes it is only when we hit rock bottom that we can become motivated to act, because then we really feel that we have absolutely nothing to lose except our feeling of desperation.

Anne rewrote her self profile and this time her answers looked different. She knew which were the qualities that she would like to change and was able to specify some of the things which she felt affected her ability to communicate. 'I can't say "no", I can't make decisions, I'm afraid to stand up for myself, I've got no confidence . . . .'

When Anne brainstormed for ways to change she was amazed by her ideas. They included saying hello to her new neighbours; going to visit India, a place that she had always dreamed about; telling her son that she didn't want to spend Christmas with his family this year; returning a faulty garment to the shop; joining the WI to make more friends; telling the milkman that he overcharged her on last month's bill . . . and so the list went on and on.

Anne was surprised by her own ideas, about some of which she said, 'I didn't even know I thought that' or 'that was a dream I had over thirty years ago I had forgotten all about' or 'fancy me wanting to do that'.

Anne chose what she considered to be low-risk challenges and went away to practise some of them. As she acted, her fears started to fall away. 'Whatever was I afraid of for all those years? The only thing that I risk is failure and I can't even fail any more because every time I take a risk I feel better about myself for having had a go.'

When we contradict our fears we are in an all-win situation. There is nothing to lose but fear itself.

Look again at your self profile assessment. Have you spotlighted the areas where you would like to see change in your life? Have you brainstormed for ideas to change? *Are you ready to change?*

14.

It's Not What You See, It's the Way That You See It

Our self-esteem (or lack of it) directly affects the way we see the world. Look again at Figure 14. Are you low or high in self-esteem? Is your world view limited or expansive? Are you operating in a cycle of victim consciousness or a cycle of creative consciousness?

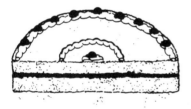 

How would you describe this cake? Is it half eaten or is there half left? Is the glass half empty or half full?

What do you believe to be true about your world? Your perceptions (beliefs, assumptions, expectations) create your view of the world.

My World View

Look at the statements below, are they true or false for you?

T/F

1. Life is difficult – we are here to struggle.
2. Nature is bountiful.
3. There is never enough of anything to go round.
4. People are basically selfish.
5. People are basically helpful and supportive.
6. Life is a drudge.
7. We can transform the planet if we really want to.
8. The world is full of sadness.
9. No obstacle is too great to overcome.
10. The world is a beautiful place.
11. It is not safe to put your trust in others.
12. We all deserve the best that life has to offer.

Look at your answers. What do they reveal about you? The questions to ask yourself are: *Does my world view work for me? Does it support creative consciousness or victim consciousness? Does it increase or decrease my self-esteem?*

I gave this exercise to some colleagues of mine. Almost all of them had a similar reaction. Robert expressed it like this.

'Look I can see what you are getting at but I must be truthful. I know which way I *should* answer the questions but I have to say what I know to be true. How can I believe that the world is a beautiful place? I'd really like to but I can only see the innate selfishness of human beings. Look at the extent of war and famine in the world. How can I believe that nature is bountiful? Believe me, people are out for what they can get. Just look at the ecology of the planet. What about the ozone layer? The proof is in front of our eyes. Yes, I believe that we are here to struggle against unsurmountable odds and there's very little we can do about it. I think it's very simplistic and naive to think otherwise.'

Robert proceeded to try to have a heated and angry discussion with me. Surely I could see the way things really are? It would be great to be able to wear rose-tinted glasses and to pretend things were OK, but how would anything change if everyone pretended that everything was hunky dory?

But how can anything change if we lose hope? We give away our creative power by believing that we are victims to a system that we cannot change. Do you remember the Law of Attraction, which states that we create whatever we think about? On whom can you blame the 'state of the world'? If you can find someone to blame, what good does it do you and what good does it do the rest of the world?

A negative world view has many limitations. It certainly doesn't make you feel good! Robert feels angry, depressed and victimized. Perhaps he has been able to absolve some personal guilt but only at the expense of his own sense of personal power and self-esteem. It doesn't effect any positive changes. Negative thoughts reinforce problems.

Maybe you feel like Robert. Perhaps you would like to believe some good, positive things about human nature but feel that in all honesty you can't. Why can't you? Where did you learn your powerful negative beliefs about the world and its inhabitants?

Mottoes – Messages from the Past

Blessed is he who expecteth nothing for he will never be disappointed . . . It never rains but it pours . . . Pride goes before a fall . . . Don't count your chickens before they are hatched . . . The grass is always greener on the other side

. . . Familiarity breeds contempt . . . All that glisters is not gold . . . Take care, good folk are scarce . . .

As a child I held great reverence for proverbs. They seemed to be the embodiment of great pearls of wisdom which were handed down through the generations. As soon as my daughter was old enough to appreciate their subtleties I took on my role in passing on these immortal words. As a grown-up who was somewhat bewildered by the world it was at least a relief to have some 'home truths' to rely upon.

When I became interested in the way that thought patterns affect the quality of our lives, I began to investigate the ways in which we learn our beliefs. It wasn't long before I was taking a closer look at proverbs.

Each proverb contains some possible grains of truth but this does not mean that it *quotes* the truth. If many hands make light work, why do too many cooks spoil the broth? Are cautionary tales about the sin of pride and the dangers of expectations and over friendliness really useful to us? I felt some loss when I realized that even proverbs were based on a certain way of viewing the world. Wasn't anything sacrosanct any more?

Such a large part of our social conditioning involves the important directives which we heard as a child. When I ask people if they can remember any of their family mottoes they often laugh and say that they don't come from the sort of family that has mottoes. But we are not talking about heraldic mottoes here. Every family has mottoes. Do you recognize any of these?

Be nice . . . Know your place . . . Eat everything on your plate . . . Grin and bear it . . . Don't upset anyone . . . Keep your feelings to yourself . . . Don't answer back . . . Don't ask stupid questions . . .

Have you any mottoes to add to this list? Give yourself some time to try to remember. What you have learned from your mottoes can have an important effect on the quality of your life.

But always remember that 'every cloud has a silver lining', and we are about to discover it!

15.

This is a World of Plenty

A positive world view has a lot going for it:

- It increases your self-esteem.
- It is expansive as it attracts other forms of positivity.
- It is creative: positive thoughts are an agent for conscious change.
- It makes you feel good.
- It makes everyone else feel good.

How do you feel at this moment? ....

How are you reacting to these statements? ....

Creating a Vision

Before we go any further I want you to put all your negativity into this box.

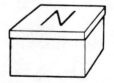

This is a picture of your negativity box. After we have finished creating a vision you may open the box and take back your negativity. I'm not asking you to stop having negative beliefs; I only want you to suspend them for a while.

Open the box, put your negativity inside and put the lid back on. Don't worry that you haven't done it properly / haven't put all of it in / you feel stupid / you don't want to do this any more / or whatever else you may be thinking. If you are prepared to try to use your negativity box it will work for you; your intention is all that matters. Now forget all about the box and we will start to create a vision.

Relax in a comfortable position and read the following passage.

You can hear a bird singing in the distance, its song is beautiful and clear. You can hear the bird getting closer. You look up and see a fantastic bird of paradise. It has feathers of every imaginable colour, red, blue, green, yellow, orange, purple, pink. It looks as bright as a jewel. The bird calls to you; it flies ahead and you follow. You look around and find yourself in a buttercup meadow. The sky is very blue, the grass is a beautiful green, there are buttercups everywhere, their golden cups bobbing in the light breeze. You are following a narrow path and ahead you can see some cows grazing in the distance. You have a feeling of great peace. The warm golden sun is caressing your skin. You can hear the cows mooing and the bees buzzing. This is a beautiful and safe place. The bird has stopped ahead and is sitting on a branch of a large, leafy oak tree. You sit down on the grass under the tree.

The air is fragrant with the smells of freshly mown grass and honeysuckle and lavender. You sit there, resting in the sunshine, enjoying this beautiful place and feeling deeply contented.

You can hear the gentle sound of water flowing nearby. There is a small stream running alongside your path. You can see fish swimming along in the clear water and dragonflies with their bejewelled wings of blues and greens hovering over the surface.

The bird flies on ahead and, feeling well rested, you follow. Soon you realize that your path is winding upwards towards the source of the stream at the top of the hill, and there, where the stream begins, you see a white castle shining in the sunshine. It is exquisite and looks just like a castle from a fairy tale. You feel excited and follow the bird to the entrance.

As you climb the steps of the castle you hear the sounds of beautiful music and laughter. There is a party going on inside. You know that you are welcome. In fact you know that everyone is waiting for you. As you enter everyone turns to smile at you. Everyone whom you have ever met is here. There is your family, there are your friends, there are your acquaintances, there are the people you don't like, there are your enemies... Look around at everyone – they are all smiling at you, their arms outstretched in welcome. You hear them say together, 'We have been waiting for you. You are very welcome here.'

Your heart feels full of joy and happiness. Wander around the castle and enjoy the hospitality . . . There is an abundance of everything, more than plenty for everyone.

Then you see the bird again. It flies ahead and asks you to follow. You climb the castle staircase and discover, at the very top of the stairs, a huge roomful of treasures. Look at the jewels, the beautiful clothes, the gold and silver, enjoy the opulence. There is so much of everything. The bird asks you to take a gift. You can choose anything in the room. You choose your gift. Now you leave the treasure chamber and go back down the stairs, passing all the familiar faces. People are shaking your hand and saying goodbye. You feel very warm towards everyone. As you reach the castle entrance you turn for one last look. Everyone is smiling at you as they say together, 'Come back whenever you wish. We will always be here'.

You are feeling contented and happy as you step from the castle into the bright, warm sunshine.

The bird flies ahead as you take the winding path to the bottom of the hill. You walk slowly alongside the stream, carrying your gift from the castle, until you reach the oak tree. The bird settles in the branches of the tree and you rest against its trunk. Look around at the golden buttercups. See the cows in the distance. Smell the grass, the lavender and the honeysuckle. This is a beautiful and tranquil place and you feel safe and happy. You know that you can always come to this place to rest and become refreshed. Everyone whom you have ever met will always be here to welcome you whenever you wish to return.

At your feet you see a box. This is your treasure box. Take your gift and put it inside the treasure box.

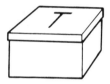

You know now that this journey is over. You are ready to go home happy and contented. Return slowly. Rub your hands together, stretch and feel yourself coming back into your body.

When you have read through the instructions a couple of times you will be ready to create a vision for yourself. Relax completely and this time close your eyes and take yourself on the journey. Give yourself time to enjoy all your experiences along the way.

How do you feel after the journey? ....

The full effects of the visualization take a while to be felt and so it is a good idea to give yourself a complete break from the book. Close the book now and come back to it in twenty-four hours. *Give yourself a break. You deserve it.*

Which Box Will You Open?

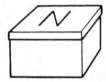 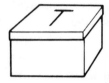

Twenty four hours later and how are you feeling? ....

You can never open both boxes at the same time. If your negativity box is open then your treasure box remains locked. If your treasure box is open your negativity box is locked. The boxes are mutually exclusive.

Which box will you open at this moment?

We all know what happens when we hold negative beliefs, but what happens when we hold our treasure? Our treasure is the gift we have brought back from our journey. When we hold our treasure we are reminded of the feelings which we experienced in the beautiful place of our vision. We feel safe, contented, peaceful, relaxed, happy and loved. We experience the abundance of our universe. We feel good and so we attract the good. We are operating in a cycle of creative consciousness and we are high in self-esteem.

We have seen many ways in which we have been taught our negative beliefs and now we have learned how negative thought patterns can be dissolved.

Negative belief + Negative vision =
Negative thought pattern

New affirmation + Creative vision =
New positive thought pattern

Whenever you find yourself holding a negative thought you can use this technique – it will always work! If your visions and beliefs aren't working for you then you are a victim of your own thought patterns. Make a new positive affirmation, create a new vision and change your thought pattern so that it supports you.

Remember that you love and value yourself and that you deserve the best that life has to offer!

When I first came across the idea of replacing my negative beliefs with positive beliefs I made lots of personal validating affirmations. I repeated the statements which you have been asked to make earlier in the book – 'I deserve emotional support', 'I love and value myself'. These affirmations always made me feel good about myself but I noticed a feeling of guilt creeping in. I didn't understand why I felt guilty until I began to say, 'I deserve the best that life has to offer'. A repeated reaction to this statement was a feeling of 'Why me? Why do I deserve so much when many people have so little. If I have something it means that someone else has to do without.'

And so I felt guilty! I am mentioning this personal reaction because I have found it to be a really common response. We all know that feelings of guilt don't make us feel good and yet what do we do with them? Where do they come from? Eventually I unearthed the problem. I held a very strong belief that 'there is never enough of anything to go round' and so, if I have something, it means that someone else is deprived. Do you believe in scarcity?

We have learned to believe in scarcity. There's not enough food to go round / not enough water / not enough money / not enough time / not enough love . . . Of course we believe in scarcity. It's everyone for themselves in this competitive and warlike world . . . or is it? What happens if we believe in a world of plenty?

'There is plenty of everything to go round.' How do you feel when you make this statement? Do you think it isn't true?

It is true! Our combined belief in scarcity ensures that people starve in one part of the world whilst food is stock-piled or destroyed in another part of the world. Is this really a question of scarcity?

How can I say that the world is full of plenty when the sea is becoming poisoned, when whole species of plants and animals are being wiped out, when the very air we breathe is becoming poisoned? But where is this 'scarcity' coming from? *We have created scarcity – let's create abundance instead.*

Creating New Thought Patterns

'*This is a world of plenty.*' This is a positive affirmation which contradicts our belief in scarcity. You can make this statement in whichever ways you like – say it, sing it, write it . . . express it in some way.

Affirmation of abundance + Creative vision of abundance = Belief in abundance

We have seen that a new affirmation plus a creative vision can dissolve a negative thought pattern.

When we went on our journey we created a vision of abundance. Just close your eyes and see your castle of plenty. Go in and experience again that feeling of being completely welcome. Look at everyone smiling at you. There is an abundance of affection here, there is more than enough to go round. Look at the gorgeous clothes, the beau-tiful jewels, the wonderful food . . . you see that there is more than enough for everyone.

The more often you say an affirmation and support it with a creative vision, the quicker you will be able to change your thought patterns. If you create a belief in abundance you will attract abundance. (Remember that we live in a magnetic field.) *If we all created abundance in our lives there would be no room for scarcity.*

This technique, of affirming and creating a vision, can be used effectively to change any belief which isn't working for you.

Perhaps there is something which you would like to do but feel you can't because you are 'not good enough'. Apply the technique. Make your affirmation:

I am a successful ....

I am good at ....

I find it easy to ....

Create an affirmation which is suitable for you. Maybe you would like to name yourself in the affirmation:

I .... am an excellent ....

Be creative, say whatever feels good to you.

Now *see* yourself being good at .... or as an excellent .... Close your eyes and picture the scene. See yourself being a successful .... You look so confident and relaxed. Feel what it is like to be a successful.................................... See people treating you with the respect which you deserve. Make the vision as real as you can, let your imagination take you where it will. How are you feeling at this moment?

If you have any negative feelings just let them go. Whenever we work to change our thought patterns we are challenging beliefs which we have held for a long time. As we are releasing our negativity we sometimes feel it very strongly. If this happens to you just remember that this feeling will pass quickly. Just keep on affirming and creating your vision.

You can use these techniques to create change in all areas of your life. Just *say* what you would like to happen and then *see* it happening.

There are only three rules but they are most important:

1. *The affirmation must be a positive statement.* It is no good saying something like 'I am not a boring person'. The belief that you are boring will remain unless it is contradicted by a *positive* statement about yourself such as, 'I am an interesting person'.

2. *The affirmation must be made in the present tense.* If I affirm that, 'I am going to enjoy a life of prosperity' it will always stay beyond my grasp. I have stated that I am 'going to' have something and that is how the situation will stay. My belief belongs to the future and will always remain there. I need to rephrase the statement to bring the belief into the here and now. I could say, 'I am enjoying a life of prosperity'.

3. *You must be able to feel that your affirmation is possible.* Your belief is all important.

Would you like to try making an affirmation? Write down your affirmation. Read it to yourself. Say it out loud. Look in the mirror and say it to yourself. Create a vision which supports your affirmation. See your affirmation in action. Feel the positive feelings. Live your affirmation in glorious technicolour. Creating new thought patterns is amazing fun. Enjoy yourself!

An Expansive World View

> Two men looked out through their prison bars.
> One saw mud
> The other saw stars.

If you are stuck with the mud then you have become a victim of your own belief system. If your world view is limited in this way then your lifestyle is one based on fear. Why look at the mud if you can look at the stars?

By creating a belief in the plentiful nature of our universe

we can develop an expansive world view. This way of looking at the world supports our self-esteem and so enables us
to 'make things happen' in our lives. We can initiate the
action rather than just providing a reaction. Look back at
Figure 5 on page xvi. If we have high self-esteem we are not
afraid to act. We know how to communicate our wishes; we
know when and how to say 'no'; and we are able to be flexible and creative. In other words, we possess various important skills.

Contrary to popular belief, there is no luck attached to
whether we have these skills or not. Maybe it is more difficult for some people to express themselves clearly. Perhaps
you feel that you are the sort of person who just *can't* say
'no'. Happily for us the fact remains that these skills are just
that, they are abilities which can be learned.

If you are a victim you believe that you can't learn these
skills, you are not *that* sort of person – your self-esteem is
low and falling. However, if you are responding creatively,
you are working on improving your self-esteem. You are
prepared to keep an open mind and to try to learn the techniques. Your belief in yourself and your self-esteem is rising.

If we can't communicate our needs to others how will
they know how to respond? If we say 'yes' when we mean
'no' how can we expect anyone to realize that we didn't
really mean what we said? If we can't say what we want we
will never get what we want.

If we are able to express ourselves clearly to others we
have a much greater chance of achieving our desired result.

If we can communicate our needs whilst also remaining
sensitive to the needs of others, it is highly likely that we
will achieve our desired outcome. However, even if we fail,
our self-esteem can remain intact – we know that we did the
very best we could and we can't always win.

The following chapters contain techniques which will help
you to put your personal action plan into operation. *Don't
react – just act.*

16.

Decision Making

> Even more than we are doers, we are deciders. Once our decision is clear the doing becomes effortless, for then the universe supports and empowers our action.
>
> Ralph Blum, *Book of Runes*

What is the difference between people who make things happen and those who seem unable to initiate anything? Why can one person create new directions for themself whilst another always appears to be victimized by circumstances?

The difference lies in their ability to make decisions.

How do you feel about making decisions? Would you describe your decision making powers as:

- Good
- Not so good
- Poor
- Can't decide.

Many people find decision making difficult because they feel unable to trust their own judgement. This lack of trust is self perpetuating – see Figure 15. We have seen many times how this negative downward spiral works.

As we start to clear away our personal energy blocks, our

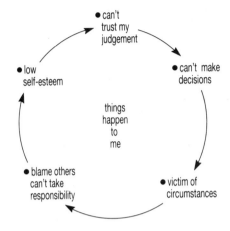

Figure 15   *The 'things happen to me' spiral*

self-esteem rises and our decision-making powers improve. As we start to express our feelings instead of suppressing them we begin to take charge of our own lives and so learn to respect our own judgement. However we can also alter the 'things happen to me' spiral by working directly on the decision-making process.

IDA

IDA is a simple formula which you can use whenever you are uncertain about what to decide and therefore how to act. IDA represents the following process:

Intention ⎯⎯⎯⎯⎯► Decision ⎯⎯⎯⎯⎯► Action

I cannot act if I can't decide how to act. I can't make a decision unless I know what I intend to happen. If action is the flower, then intention is the seed of that flower.

To discover your intention you ask yourself this question: *'What do I want to happen?'* This is a powerful and assertive question. As you define your intention so you define your action.

- Think of an area in your life where you would like to see a change.
- Now discover your intention.

Ask yourself, 'What do I want to happen?' Write down your answers. Remember that the effectiveness of your action is totally dependent upon the clarity of your intention. Be as specific as you can when you answer this question.

Emma is unhappy at work. She has worked in a shoe shop for six years and she says that she is 'sick of the smell of feet'. In the school holidays she has to make complicated and expensive childcare arrangements and every night after school the children are alone for two hours until she gets home. There are many reasons for Emma to change her job, but will she be able to do so?

I asked Emma what she wanted to happen but she found this question difficult to answer. She was able to write a long list of things that she *didn't* want to happen but said, 'I can't think of anything that I want to happen'. This is not an unusual state of affairs. Many people experience a lifetime of unhappiness because they are unable to decide what it is that they want in life. This inability stems from lack of practice. If you don't use your legs the muscles will wither away. If you don't exercise your decision-making powers they too will waste away. Very soon, a person who *doesn't* make decisions turns into a person who *can't* make decisions. Again, it is all a question of belief. Emma finds it impossible to say what she wants because, basically, she doesn't believe that she can change her circumstances.

Ruth drove a delivery van for an electronics firm. She said, 'The job bores me silly and the hours don't suit my family at all.' When I asked her what she wanted to happen she was full of ideas. She knew that she wanted to change her job. (She obviously believed that this was possible.) I asked her what sort of job she wanted. She said that she had thought a lot about this and had written down all her job requirements. These included:

- Hours to suit school hours
- Intellectual stimulation
- Working with others.

Ruth was able to specify her intention and this made it possible for her to plan her future. She went to see a careers counsellor who suggested that she trained to be a teacher. Ruth was thrilled by this idea and said that she would never have thought of it herself. The question, 'What do I want to happen?' generates some magic. If you can believe in yourself enough to answer this question then you can open up all sorts of new possibilities.

Ruth has nearly qualified as a teacher. Emma still works in the shop. It is obviously vitally important that you can express your intention as specifically as possible.

Look at your own example. What replies did you make to the question? It's a good idea to use the 'brainstorming' technique here. Write down anything which comes to mind even if it appears irrelevant. Just allow yourself to express everything that comes, without judging its validity – new ideas often emerge with this technique.

If you are still having difficulties, support yourself with an affirmation. Think of something appropriate such as, 'I make things happen', or 'I know what I want'. Remember to make affirmations positive and to keep them in the present tense.

Reinforce your intention by using all the techniques you know. Make your intention real by:

- Visualizing your intention – *see* your outcome in action.

- Affirming that your outcome is happening – *believe* in your goal.

When you have a clear idea of what you want to happen you can then make some decisions. To clarify your decisions you ask the question, '*How do I make it happen?*' The answers to this question will determine the actions you must take. Brainstorm for ideas and then make your decisions real by *seeing* yourself putting them into action.

When your decisions are clear you are ready for *action* and appropriate action depends upon effective communication.

Simon is being bullied by his supervisor at work. He enjoys his job and doesn't want to leave. He uses the IDA process to enable himself to take control of this situation.

- *Intention.*
    - To keep his job, which will mean changing the nature of the relationship between him and his supervisor.
- *Decisions.*
    - To show the supervisor that he will no longer be treated badly.
    - To stand up for himself and not to be so frightened of authority figures.
- *Action.*
    - To communicate his meaning clearly. This includes not saying 'yes' when he means 'no'.
    - To allow himself to take some risks and be more assertive. After all, things can't be much worse than they are now.
    - To leave his job if the new tactics don't work – it's not worth bashing his head against a brick wall. He will never be happy if he isn't treated properly.

And so Simon has formulated a plan of action, and central to this plan is the idea of effective communication.

We communicate our self-esteem (or lack of it) to others

by our words and actions. We teach people how to treat us. If I am low in self-esteem I will very effectively communicate that message to you. I expect to be treated badly and so I will feel hard done by, however hard you try to treat me well. If I am high in self-esteem I expect there to be mutual respect between you and me. If victims and victimizers enter my life they either leave very quickly or change their behaviour. I do not support victim-type behaviour.

If you feel like one of life's victims and you want to change, use IDA to discover *how*:

- *Intention*. Specify your intention to increase your self-esteem.
- *Decision*. Decide how you need to change your behaviour.
- *Action*. Change your behaviour by acting differently.

17.

Changing Your Behaviour

Why Are You Waiting?

You have specified your intention, made your decision and you are ready to act – what are you waiting for?

I'll do it next year . . . when the children are older . . . when I'm feeling braver . . . when I win the pools . . . when I've had some more training . . . when he / she notices me . . . when I'm appreciated . . . when I'm forgiven . . . when I've lost some weight . . . when I have a settled relationship . . . when he / she says it's OK . . . when the weather improves . . . when I fall in love . . . and so the excuses roll on. We can all come up with lots of reasons *not* to act.

Making changes involves risk taking. I use the term 'risk taking' to mean daring to make changes in your behaviour. The risks involved are not of the life-threatening type. We all have our own personal habitual behaviour patterns which are holding us back. These patterns are limiting but oh so comfortable; they are like a favourite piece of old clothing which is very cosy but falling to pieces. If we want to make things happen we must dare to change the way we behave and this means being able to ask for what we want.

It *is* a risky business

- What if I fail?
- What if I am rejected?
- What if he / she won't like me any more?

What if I never take a risk and so remain a victim of my own fear for the rest of my life? Risk taking has a direct relationship with self-esteem. If I am playing the victim I make sure that I am never ultimately responsible for anything. I won't take any initiatives and so I can guarantee that I can never fail – I can always blame someone else. My self concept is poor, I have very low expectations and I perpetuate these negative beliefs by not daring to change. My self-esteem is low and still falling.

As you dare to risk changing, so your self-esteem will rise. So what if you do fail / are rejected / he/she doesn't like you any more? What have you got to lose? Are you really prepared to sacrifice the quality of your life in order to appease other people? Do other people's opinions mean that much to you? When you are frightened to act just ask yourself this question: 'What is the worst thing that can happen to me?' The answer is often surprisingly trivial.

So you have decided to take a risk! You are going to do something different. The success of your actions depends less on *what* you are doing and more on *how* you do it.

It Ain't What You Do, It's The Way That You Do It

Figure 16 represents the range of responses which are open to us when we interact with others. We can either respond with creative behaviour or with victim behaviour. These choices are mutually exclusive: at any one time we can operate in only one mode or the other. If our self-esteem is high we can make creative responses and if it is low we respond as victims.

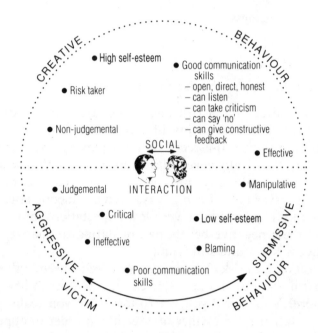

Figure 16   *Types of behaviour*

Victim behaviour can be aggressive or submissive or somewhere in between or even a mixture of the two. Although
none of us can be categorized according to type, we may
recognize some of our own behaviour patterns by looking at
the model of behaviour described in the diagram.

Imagine the following situation.

Your elderly father lives alone a long way from you. You
have always had a difficult relationship with him and as he
has aged he has become even more perverse. Your father
comes to stay with you twice a year and you feel that these
visits are about as much as you can handle. During his visits
you find yourself taking a mediating role in order to keep
the peace. Fireworks fly when your father and your children
are under the same roof. Your partner is very supportive but
you know that s/he finds your father very difficult. Your

own brothers and sisters keep away from their father as much as possible. They all agree that you are very patient with him and that you know just how to handle him. They never invite him to stay with them. At a Christmas reunion of all the family, your father tells everyone that he is lonely and depressed and that he is only waiting for you to offer him a permanent home and then he will be happy. Everyone turns to look at you.

How do you think that you would respond?

Below are three possible options which demonstrate some elements of the aggressive, submissive and creative styles of behaviour.

Aggressive

How can I possibly have you here, there isn't enough room. Anyway even if there was I couldn't handle putting up with your moods, and why should I? Why am I the only one who will look after you? I think that it's about time that one of your other children did something for you. Why don't you ask them to help you for a change.

Submissive

Oh dear, well I suppose you do need somewhere to stay. I wish one of the others could offer to have you but I don't expect they can. I'm sure we will be able to settle down together somehow. If only the house was bigger, it might be easier. I suppose I should have asked you before but I wasn't quite sure how we would all manage. Oh well, I expect that we will manage somehow.

Creative

Well dad, I'm sorry to hear that you are feeling so miserable and obviously we must discuss all your options to see what we can do to help. Unfortunately we haven't enough space to have you here as you know. I'm sure that one of the others would be delighted to help. Why don't you discuss it with them first before we start looking at the alternative possibilities.

How did you reply to your ageing father? Which style did you adopt?

At first glance aggressive and submissive behaviour appear to be totally different. The aggressor is loud and dominating and may appear to be determined and confident whilst the submissive person is quieter and seems to be lacking in direction and confidence. However, the two behavioural styles share many features. They are both manipulative, critical and blaming and they are both equally ineffective.

If I feel pressurized by you (and I adopt the aggressive style of behaviour) I will attack you verbally and my body language will be equally threatening. I use these tactics to frighten my 'adversaries' into submission, and this often works in the short term.

Think of a time when you were beaten into submission by an aggressive person. How did you feel? What sort of relationship (if any) do you have with that person now?

Aggressive behaviour is alienating. It closes down all possibility of cooperation and communication because it is mutually invalidating. If I am an aggressor I create victims and in so doing I become a victim myself. I am mistrusting and fearful of others and I am very low in self-esteem.

If I am a submissive person and I am feeling threatened I withdraw immediately into victim-type behaviour. I feel hard done by and sorry for myself. Often the aggressive and submissive styles of behaviour attract each other – the two types make a beautiful couple. Can you think of two people who you know who act out these supporting roles?

In my submissive role I may initially press your guilt buttons as you try to help in some way. You soon discover however that I don't want rescuing. I would rather keep moaning and blaming as this ensures that I never have to make any decisions – everything can always be someone else's fault. I feel safe in my role as a victim and I use this position to victimize others. This type of behaviour also denies any meaningful negotiation and communication. Because I am submissive I am afraid to express myself; I don't trust others because I can't trust myself; I am self critical and so I criticize others; and I have no self respect and little or no self-esteem.

Do you recognize any of these behaviour patterns? Do you know people who operate in the aggressive or submissive mode? We have all experienced being both aggressive and submissive. When our self-esteem is low we can only operate in the victim mode. Notice, in the figure, that there is a two-way arrow between aggressive and submissive behaviour. We often tend to swing between these extremes and this is particularly true for women. The need for women to break out from their traditionally held submissive role has frequently resulted in a swing towards aggression, in an attempt to alter the balance of power between the sexes. Of course, as we have seen, the aggressor is also a victim. Aggressive behaviour only alienates people; it doesn't create any positive changes. Many women discover this to their cost and, in the throes of guilt, swing back apologetically into the submissive role. This constant swinging backwards and forwards is confusing, uncomfortable, and ultimately self defeating.

Personal freedom, or the lack of it, has nothing to do with feelings of superiority (aggression) or inferiority (submission). It is linked directly with self-esteem. We are only free when we stop indulging in victim behaviour and begin responding creatively. Creative behaviour requires that we communicate in a direct and honest way. We need to be able to express our needs to others whilst remaining sensitive to their feelings. When we are communicating in this way we are respecting others and respecting ourselves. Our feelings of self worth are supported and we are reinforcing our self-esteem.

Creative behaviour is totally unlike victim behaviour. It is non-manipulative and non-judgemental. It is effective and it reinforces high self-esteem. We can all *learn* to respond creatively so long as we are prepared to risk changing our behaviour.

All we need to do is to learn the skills of good communication. These include: learning to say 'no'; learning to listen; learning to deal with criticism; and learning to give constructive feedback.

18.

'No' is not a Dirty Word

Of course I'll look after your six children . . . I'd love to cook dinner for ten people tonight . . . Yes I'll take the encyclopedias; I'm sure we can find room for another set . . . Of course I'll pick up the children from the disco at 11pm . . . Of course I don't mind . . . . . . Of course I *do* mind . . . I'm absolutely furious with everyone. How *dare* they keep asking me to do these things? . . . Why is it always me who gets lumbered? . . . Why does everyone put me in this position? . . . What have I done to deserve it?

It is really more a question of what I haven't done. The ability to become a victim is closely linked with the inability to say 'no'. Can you remember when you last agreed to do something that you didn't want to do? How did you feel as you were being asked? How did you act? Why didn't you say 'no'?

The maintenance of high self-esteem depends upon our ability to communicate our meaning clearly. If we say 'yes' when we mean 'no' then we are denying our own needs and inviting people to victimize us. Why do we find it so hard to say 'no'? Why will some people do almost anything to avoid saying this word.

Saying 'no' is a problem for most people because the

word is emotively linked with personal rejection. The key word here is 'rejection'. We have learned a set of beliefs which associates saying the word 'no' with behaviour that is described as uncaring, thoughtless, hard, unfeeling, mean . . . and so on. 'If you say "no" to me I will feel personally rejected and threatened by you. I depend on your good opinion of me.' Similarly, 'If I say "no" to you, you will feel rejected and you won't like me any more.' If I am low in self-esteem I am totally at the mercy of the opinion of others. If you don't like me then I am worthless. Small wonder that we experience such a mixed bag of emotions when we want to say 'no' – it seems that our sense of self worth is always on the line.

To feel rejected is to be victimized. The victim's 'no' stems from this feeling of personal rejection – it can be submissive, aggressive or anywhere in between.

The 'Submissive No'

You ask me if I can give you a lift into town tomorrow. I don't want to because I've planned to do something else. We are friends but I am unable to say 'no' to you because I am a victim of a limiting set of beliefs. My self concept is poor and is based on a host of ideas about what I 'should', 'can't' and 'must' do . . . If only I could say 'no', but I can't! My major preoccupation is, 'What do people think about me?' and I will do anything to ensure that people will like me. I use the 'submissive no' and it is totally ineffective; in fact it hardly exists. When I use the 'submissive no' I don't actually say 'no', I usually say 'yes', but I really mean 'no'. I wish people would realize that when I say 'yes' I usually mean 'no'. People take advantage of me and I don't think it's fair. Sometimes I use the 'indirect no', but it is also ineffective and it gets me into all sorts of trouble. It works like this.

Although I have no intention of giving you a lift I say that I'll try to reorganize things so that I can. This means that I can delay saying 'no' for as long as possible and it also ensures that you won't have time to ask anyone else for a lift.

All the variations of the 'submissive no' ensure that, if I must be a victim of your request, then you will also be a victim. You will become a casualty, either of my resentment (I may have said 'yes' but I really meant 'no') or of my 'indirect no' (I won't help but I won't tell you until it's too late). The 'submissive no' is not a clear and honest response as it denies any communication which is based on trust. Everyone involved becomes a victim which means low self-esteem all round.

The 'Aggressive No'

I have also assimilated many authoritarian, childhood directives. My belief system is full of 'shoulds' and 'ought tos' but this doesn't make it hard for me to say 'no'. I believe that you 'should' say what you mean without beating about the bush. You ask me for a lift and I give you a straight 'no'. I don't care what you think and if you don't like it you can lump it. This approach can hurt. Remember how we link 'no' with rejection. The aggressive line denies that we have feelings which can be hurt and so if I use the hard, aggressive approach this ensures that I can never be hurt. Of course, in truth, everyone will be hurt. When we invalidate ourselves and each other our self-esteem is low, we have no self respect and we feel frightened and unsupported. Actually of course I really do care what people think about me, that's why I make such a big thing about not caring.

The 'victim's no' certainly takes us round the houses and back again. What an incredible waste of effort is involved in this totally ineffective approach. How does it feel to be on the receiving end of a victim's 'no'?

- Can you think of a time when someone said 'yes' to you when you knew that they really wanted to say 'no'? How did it feel?
- How about being on the receiving line of an 'indirect no'. How does this feel?
- What does it feel like to be hit with an 'aggressive no'?

High self-esteem is linked directly with good communication skills. If you want to make things happen then you must know how to ask for what you want. You also need to know how to make things *not* happen, if you don't want them to. The victim's 'no' springs from feelings of low self-esteem; the person saying 'no' in this way is muddled and unable to open the lines of communication. When we are on the receiving end of the victim's 'no' we also become muddled.

What does she really mean? . . . Look it's really OK if you can't manage it . . . She says that she will try to do it but I've a feeling that she won't and then it will be too late to ask anyone else . . . I wish I hadn't asked her . . . Well I don't mind straight talking but she could have told me why she said 'no', she was very hurtful . . .

The 'Creative No'

The 'victim's no' derives from limiting beliefs about self and the world. We have looked many times at the power of our beliefs and we know that they can be changed if they don't work for us.

When we are ready to let go of our restricting beliefs, we are no longer responding as victims and we are free to use the 'creative no'. This is an assertive response to a request which we want to refuse. Before we can use the 'creative no' we need to be able to de-sensitize ourselves to any feelings of emotional rejection which we may experience when we hear or say the word 'no'. The following may help.

● Try this affirmation: *'I find it easy to say "no".'* Say it as often as you can.

● Look at these statements:
  – 'When I say "no" to you it just means that I don't want to do what you are asking. It does not mean that I am rejecting you as a person.'
  – 'When you say "no" to me it only means that you don't want to do what I am asking. It does not mean that you are personally rejecting me.'

● Take your understanding of these statements into your life. When you are afraid to say 'no', think about the true meaning of your communication. Remember that you are not rejecting the other person. When someone says 'no' to you and you go into an emotional spin, remember that they are not rejecting you, they are only saying 'no' to your request.

When we feel rejected we feel victimized. When we act as victims our self-esteem is low and still falling. Contradict your rejection response by changing your way of thinking. 'No' is not a dirty word but it is often a very necessary one. If it is both difficult to hear and to say, then we need to discover ways to make it easier.

Start by making a note of your own feelings about saying 'no'. When is it particularly hard for you – at work, at home, with strangers, with friends, with authority figures? . . . Discover where your greatest difficulties lie. How do you feel at those times? Do you feel threatened / frightened / unsure / insecure . . . ? Whatever you feel try to become aware of it.

We can use the Intention Decision Action approach to clarify our ideas when we are working on using the 'creative no'.

You have asked me to give you a lift tomorrow and I'm doing something else. Instead of muddling along in a victimized fashion I want to take control of this situation.

Intention

What is my intention here? What are you asking of me? What sort of commitment will it mean? Do I need some time to think about my answer? What do I really want to happen? Do I want to say 'no'? These simple questions are very important. If we don't ask them we will be trapped in the net of the victim's 'no'.

This is what I want to happen. I don't want to give you a lift. I do want us to remain friends. I want to say 'no' to you and I want us both to feel good after I have said 'no'.

Decision

I am going to say 'no' to you in a way which conveys my meaning and yet is not designed to be hurtful. I am reminding myself that it's OK to say 'no' to you. I am not rejecting you. I will be as sensitive as possible but if you still feel rejected I can't do anything about it. I won't change my mind and try to back down. I am going to say what I mean and I hope that you will accept my 'no' in the way that it is given.

Decision making is very important. At this stage we can think about *how* to say 'no' (there are a variety of ways as we shall see) and we can anticipate some possible reactions. We need to be ready not to back down. It is so easy to start feeling guilty. Remember that this is a refusal = rejection response.

Action

Communicate clearly even if you are nervous. You will improve with practice. The wonderful thing about learning to say 'no' is that *the more you do it the easier it gets.*

Watch that your body language is as assertive as your message. Don't give yourself away when you are at this stage. At first you will be 'pretending and practising'. This may feel strange but sometimes this is the only way to leave behind old behaviour patterns.

Stick at it. As soon as you have said 'no' once, in a situation where you have been unable to do so before, you have broken new ground. Next time it will be easier because you will have been there before.

Be ready for the reaction. Use affirmations if you feel your resolve weakening. If you feel sorry or guilty remember your intention. Don't apologize for your position: this will weaken your stand. *Keep practising!*

Some Different Ways to Say 'No'

Once you have decided that you want to say 'no', it's just a case of finding the best way to say it. Choose the approach which is most suitable. Perhaps you are dealing with a salesperson and need to let them know that you are not going to change your mind. Maybe you are speaking to someone who is easily hurt – you may find that you want to explain to this person why it is that you have to say 'no'. Perhaps you have to say 'no' to a close friend and feel the need to express how difficult it is for you to do so. Sometimes you want to compromise. You may not be able to do the job now but could do it later. You may not feel able to do that but you may be happy doing this.

Whichever way you choose, just remember a few golden

rules. It's OK to say 'no'. Speak firmly and clearly. Watch
your body language. Remind yourself of your intention if
you feel yourself weakening. If the other person feels
rejected then that really is their problem. If you say 'sorry' it
may weaken your position. Excusing and explaining are different things – explain yourself if you wish but never excuse
yourself. *Silence* is a powerful tool – use it. (You may need
to practise this.)

- Repeat the same statement – 'No I don't want to buy this
  car / go out with you / pick up your dirty washing'. This
  is a useful technique when dealing with persistent people.
  Keep repeating the same statement; it's unnerving and it
  helps to keep you on track.

- Express your feelings and then say 'no' – 'Look I'm finding this quite hard to say but I'm sure you will understand
  that my answer must be "no".'

- Say 'no' followed by an explanation. 'No I won't be able
  to work late tonight, it's too short notice. I will need to
  know at least two days in advance if you want me to stay
  late.' Only offer an explanation if it will be helpful, not if
  it is an excuse in disguise.

- Say 'no' and offer an alternative. 'I can't come tomorrow
  but I can come next week.'

- Restate the request and then say 'no'. 'I know how important it is for you to go to this all-night party but I am not
  going to let you go.' (Children are amazingly persistent in
  the face of the most unequivocal 'no'. Whichever 'no' you
  choose you will need to use a repetitive approach!)

- Say 'no' and be silent. You may find this technique
  uncomfortable at first but if you can stick it out it is really
  very effective.

Whichever technique you use there will always be a place
for silence. Eventually, once you have said your piece there
is absolutely nothing else to say. If you keep talking after

this point your position will be weakened. When you are waiting in silence for the other person to accept your 'no' remind yourself of your intention. Remember that you are not rejecting them. *You are only saying 'no'.*

19.

Listening – A Dying Art

At the station we were a team of 20 to 30 people and Yaba Walaga was able to identify many of them by their footsteps, as well as a multitude of other sounds in the cacophony of the rain forest. This highly differentiating acoustic perception is an ability totally lost in western cultures. We have also lost sight of the psychological value of the greeting and the social value of communication generally. Simple human conversation is a disappearing social phenomenon. Most oral information is now fed into electronic devices or written on machines. Most of what we hear and see emanates from the same type of technological media.

Andreas Fuglesang, *About Understanding*

What is the art of listening? What does it involves? Why is it important for good communication? The Chinese verb 'to listen' is composed of five characters, meaning:

- ear
- you
- eyes
- undivided attention
- heart.

This translation suggests that listening is more than just

hearing, which we often regard as an instinctive function. In fact the art of listening involves *all* our being. When we listen with our whole selves we are doing so much more than just hearing the words. We become aware of what is being communicated at all levels of our being – we are listening with our head and heart. When we listen to someone with *all* our attention we are validating them. We are saying, 'I respect your views / feelings / thoughts, you have a right to them and you have a right to express them.'

If you listen in the Chinese sense you are *listening to understand*; you are listening with every part of your being, with your mind / body / spirit / emotions.

When two people are listening to understand each other they are, in effect, saying to each other, you deserve my undivided attention. The lines of communication are open and both people are validating each other. They are aware of each other's self worth and so have created a truly supportive interaction. Their communication is based on trust and so can be open and honest. When we validate each other in this way we are increasing our own and each other's self-esteem.

Who is your favourite person, the one you turn to when things get rough? What are the qualities which make this person so understanding? Do they include an ability to listen? I expect that they do. Think of a time when someone really listened to you, with every part of their being. How did you feel?

....

Now what about your least favourite person? The last person you would turn to in distress. What are his / her qualities? I expect that poor listening skills is one of them.

Remember a time when you were badly listened to. How did you feel?

....

Do You Listen to Understand?

How do you listen when you are bored? Do you cut off and start daydreaming? What happens if you disagree with someone. Can you still listen to them or are you busy working out what your response will be and how you are going to say it? How does it feel when you know that someone is involved in their own thoughts when you are trying to communicate with them? Do you maintain eye contact when you are listening or are you apt to fidget and look away? Do you ever finish sentences for people? How do you feel when someone does that to you? Are you aware of a person's body language when they are talking to you? Can you listen with your eyes? If someone says one thing but contradicts it with his / her body language can you pick up these clues? If, for example, someone says that she's feeling fine but shows anxiety in her physical body – clenched fists, hunched shoulders, lack of eye contact – which would you believe? Can you listen without judgement?

Can you listen with your whole self?

We were born to listen in this way. Watch the way that babies listen. They are wholly attentive and aware. We lose these skills as we grow up and start to close up emotionally. Victim behaviour includes poor communication skills. If we are poor listeners we are responding as victims.

Our early communication experiences have a direct effect on our listening skills.

Stuart remembers that when he was a child he always spoke very quickly to his father in order to stop him interrupting and criticizing. Stuart often finds himself interrupting others and repeating his father's behaviour – he has learned to listen aggressively.

On the other hand, William, who remembers being listened to in a similar way, has become a submissive listener. He is so worried about his own performance that he doesn't have time to listen to another person and so he cuts off.

Aggressive listening may include interrupting / fidgeting / threatening body language and critical intervention. The listener's underlying message to the speaker is, 'You're not worth listening to', and so the speaker feels low in self-esteem. The lines of communication close as the speaker feels threatened and responds in a more guarded way. Aggressive listening is a victim response. We cannot respect our own sense of self worth whilst we are denying the worth of others.

The underlying message in submissive listening is, 'How am I coming over, what sort of impression am I making? I haven't got any spare attention to spend on listening to you.'

Check your own childhood communication memories. Can you find a relationship between the ways that you were listened to and the ways that you now listen?

Some Listening Skills

Become aware of *how* you listen to others by practising some of the techniques of listening:

- Concentrate on the speaker.
- Maintain eye contact as much as possible.
- Listen to the content of what is being said.
- Listen to body language.
- Try not to interrupt.
- Listen for the things that are not being said.
- Keep an open mind.
- Watch your own body language. Is it open and receptive?

These are some of the areas that you can work on. You might like to concentrate on one technique at a time and see how you develop. You may want to try everything at once. Do whatever feels comfortable for you. When you become aware of the importance of listening you immediately become a better listener and the quality of your communications will increase.

If we listen with understanding we can support someone without necessarily agreeing with them. In this way we can separate a person's intrinsic self worth from their behaviour. We are *not* our behaviour; we are more than the sum of our actions. Remember how our self-esteem is linked with our ability to separate ourselves from our mistakes and the things we can't do? Well, when we are listened to with understanding we are being validated and our self-esteem is being supported. Similarly when we can listen in this way we support our own self-esteem. Supporting self-esteem opens up the lines of communication and then all things are possible, even when we disagree about opinions. Closing our ears, eyes and in fact whole selves to another person is hurtful. It denies their self worth and closes down the likelihood of communication – and then very little is possible. Remember how it feels when someone stops listening to you.

Keep practising your listening skills. Become aware of your own blocks to listening and work at removing them. A wonderful byproduct of listening to understand is that every encounter becomes interesting in some way. All communication becomes fascinating when we listen with every part of our being. We learn so much about the other person and so much about ourselves.

20.

Breaking the Pattern

'Sticks and stones may break my bones but names can never hurt me' . . . unless I let them.

You and I are having a conversation. I've been working on saying what I mean and I've been practising my listening skills. My body language shows that I am feeling relaxed and receptive and the lines of communication are wide open. I am responding creatively and my self-esteem is high. We are beginning to have a difference of opinion but I know that it need not affect our relationship – it's OK to have different beliefs. I'm feeling non-judgemental and we are still having effective communication and *then* . . . you criticize me. I feel hurt, angry, resentful, shattered and mistrustful. I stop listening and I pull back from you physically and emotionally. The lines of communication are closed. What has happened here?

None of us enjoys being criticized. It *is* hard to accept disapproval and we have looked at numerous ways in which we can become victims to others in an eternal quest for approval. Criticism hits hard and fast and is directed at our most vulnerable spots and if we cannot deal with it our self-esteem is always on the line.

Try to think of a time recently when someone criticized you.

How did you feel? .... How did you act? ....

Criticism has threatening implications. The very word sounds menacing. Our fear of criticism has its roots in our early childhood experiences. Remember how little Johnny's mother denied his positive feelings by labelling him 'unkind', 'stupid' and 'thoughtless'? Negative labels stick to us with very strong glue and critical labelling in adulthood often stirs up the feelings of invalidation that we felt during our early experiences of receiving criticism.

Many of the negative beliefs we hold about ourselves were learned by critical labelling. 'You're useless', 'You're lazy', 'You're stupid', 'You're pathetic', 'You're no good'. Can you remember hearing any negative statements like these?

Can you think of any particular negatively affirming label which you still believe to be true about you?

Unfortunately most of the authoritarian figures of our childhood (parents, relatives, teachers etc) were unskilled in the art of giving constructive feedback – they learned the critical labelling technique from adults when *they* were children. In this way patterns of learned negative behaviour are passed down through the generations.

Imagine that you are a small child. You have made a blunder and you are frightened. Then an adult appears and, looking down at you from a great height, says, 'You're hopeless'. You have been totally invalidated. You made a mistake and now you are worth nothing. Your self-esteem is in shreds and you have been frightened and intimidated. What can a small child learn from such an incident?

- Mistakes are bad.
- If I do something 'wrong' I am worthless.
- When I am afraid I get criticized.
- Criticism is a threatening experience.
- The person who criticizes is powerful.

- The person who is being criticized is powerless.
- I am being rejected.

These assumptions are reinforced each time the child is criticized. What a legacy for the invalidated child to take into adulthood! The child has become the invalidated adult who is afraid to make a mistake; feels worthless; cannot take criticism but can give it in good measure.

Next time you are being criticized, use your witness to distance you from the actual content of the criticism. Try instead to experience your feelings fully during the encounter. This may be quite difficult because your feelings may well take you quickly into your own experiences of being the small, frightened, rejected, threatened and powerless child.

This is a great exercise because it helps to de-mystify the power of criticism. You are no longer the small 'worthless' child. No one can treat you as a victim unless you allow them to. When we respond creatively we are able to separate ourselves from our behaviour. You are not your mistakes. You are you, and your behaviour is something that you do. We can learn from the mistakes we make – our mistakes are our teachers.

Have you learned to believe that mistakes are 'bad'? If so, try saying the following affirmation: *'It's OK for me to make mistakes'*.

How does it feel to make this affirmation? ....

Next time you are being criticized and you feel yourself slipping into your 'powerless child' make this affirmation. You may not remember to do this for a while – the 'powerless child' exerts a powerful effect on our being. One day you will remember, and on that day you start to be able to deal with criticism.

Whilst we remain the 'powerless child' then we are also still acting in the 'powerful adult' and here lies the true key to a change in attitude. If we are truly 'making' people in our 'factory' of the family then, as adults, we have the ability to change the set of assumptions of the small child.

When little Johnny's mother changed her approach the whole scenario became a learning experience for both mother and child. The mother gave constructive feedback rather than criticism. This differentiation between terms is important. Constructive feedback has positive connotations. It introduces the idea of giving helpful information and so implies a supportive relationship between giver and receiver. Giving constructive feedback is a creative way of dealing with a problem. This approach facilitates change and supports the self-esteem of everyone who is involved. The facts are stated, no blame is attributed and everyone can take responsibility for their own feelings.

Imagine that I find myself in conflict with you. It seems that you want one thing and I want something else. If I am low in self-esteem I will respond in the victim mode. Look again at Figure 16 on page 126. Victim responses are judgemental, critical, blaming, manipulative and ineffective. The classic victim response to conflict is to criticize, using the role of 'powerful adult' to attack the 'powerless child'. The critic blames the victim who then withdraws, together with all hope of cooperation. (Who feels like practising good communication skills with someone who brings you down?) As soon as goodwill has been withdrawn the critic then also becomes a victim; the lines of communication are closed; and conflict remains.

The difference between giving criticism and giving constructive feedback lies in approach. Table 2 gives a few examples which demonstrate the difference between the two methods.

Criticism	*Constructive feedback*
You annoy me when you don't arrive on time. You should keep your timetable together and stop wasting my time.	When you don't turn up on time I feel frustrated because my timetable is affected.
You're always taking me for granted and expecting me to do all the domestic work when you should be doing your share.	When you don't help with the housework I feel used and taken for granted.
You never give me a cuddle when I need one and you make me feel unwanted and unloved.	When you forget to show me physical affection I feel uncared for.

Table 2   *Dealing with conflict*

Next time you want to tell someone off, stop for a moment and think about how you are going to express your dissatisfaction. Would you like this person to change their behaviour? The response you get depends upon the clarity of your communication so make your meaning as clear as possible. The 'I blame you' approach will only result in further conflict. Both parties feel victimized and suffer a blow to their self-esteem. The, 'When you do that I feel like this' method, opens the way for discussion and encourages both people to acknowledge their own feelings. No one feels victimized and the lines of communication are open. Each has a chance to talk about what is happening and so self-esteem can remain intact.

As soon as we start to own our feelings instead of blaming others for them we are taking responsibility for ourselves and this increases our self-esteem. As we learn to give constructive feedback instead of criticism, we break the 'powerful adult / powerless child' pattern and this can have far-reaching effects for everyone with whom we communicate. This is how we begin to break the habit of passing on negative behaviour patterns.

Unfortunately some people will be resistant to change and however much we may work at acknowledging our own feelings they will find it impossible to do so. These people are 'blamers'; they are always victims of something or someone; and they *love* to criticize. This is their own problem and as victims they will always suffer with low self-esteem. Their attitude is not your problem. *When you are being criticized you need not be victimized.*

Changing the Way You Respond to Criticism

Your response to criticism will largely depend upon how your deal with, what Anne Dickson (in *A Woman In Your Own Right*) calls, 'your own internal critic':

> Many of us suffer from listening to the endless critical ramblings of an internal voice which is much more damning than anything we hear from the outside. With or without the help from others, our internal critic can condemn us to the psychic stocks where we sit, waiting passively for the rotten eggs and tomatoes to be thrown in our direction. Somewhere we feel we deserve no better. We feel guilty for what we have done, for who we are and so we stay cramped in the stocks. Although it is possible to get up and walk away, we often feel stuck in position.

Your 'internal critic' is the embodiment of all the negative beliefs which you hold about yourself. When we are low in self-esteem we will do anything to avoid criticism – we can't tolerate disapproval because we disapprove of ourselves and we can't stand criticism because we are self critical.

We have seen how we develop a poor self concept by hanging on to negative beliefs about ourselves. These beliefs come from the critical labelling we experienced in our childhood. Self validation will undermine all negativity. Remember the power of 'I love and value myself'? Use this affirmation whenever you find yourself being self critical.

Someone is criticizing you and you are letting all the negative labels stick to you. (Well, don't you deserve all this criticism? Aren't you a pretty worthless sort of person anyway?) And *then* you realize that you have fallen into your old self-invalidating habits. As soon as you find yourself agreeing with critical labelling, say to yourself, 'I love and value myself'. This will remind you of what is really happening.

The next thing to recall is that, 'It's OK for me to make mistakes'. We used this technique earlier to help extricate ourselves from the powerless child syndrome. It's a powerful way to stop yourself slipping into a black hole of fear and helplessness.

Now you have given yourself some space to see things in perspective you are in a position to evaluate the content of what is being said. What sort of criticism is this? Is it justified or not? Did I behave badly on that occasion? Is this person just trying to have a go at me? It is important to ask these questions. We can learn a lot from feedback from others, however badly it is offered.

If you decide that the criticism is justified you can respond as a victim or you can respond creatively.

You say to me, 'Fancy saying that to her! That was a really stupid thing to do. You *are* insensitive.'

If I say, 'Oh I know it was the wrong thing to do. I'm ever so sorry. I'm so stupid. I'm always making mistakes', I am playing the submissive victim. I endorse the criticism; my internal critic is having a field-day and my low self-esteem has fallen even further.

Of course I could play the aggressive victim and reply with more criticism. It may go something like this: 'What right have you got to criticize when everyone knows that you are as insensitive as they come.' We are in conflict. I am counter attacking because I feel threatened and neither of us is feeling good about ourselves; we are both low in self-esteem.

However, it is possible to agree with the criticism without denying your self worth. I could say in reply, 'I am sorry, it was the wrong thing to do.' If I am aware that it is a tendency of mine to be thoughtless I could even add, 'I know that I can be insensitive sometimes and I'm trying to change my approach.' These are creative responses which do not diminish your self-esteem. You can apologize without grovelling. It *is* all right to make mistakes. You may even try *asking* for constructive feedback in order to gain a different perspective. Next time you are questioning your behaviour try asking someone (whose judgement you trust) to give you some constructive feedback.

As you practise separating your self from your behaviour you will find that you take things much less personally. So you made a mistake. You can admit it, it doesn't detract from your self worth. By using an assertive approach you contradict your 'powerless child' and so strengthen your position. You can learn from your mistakes and maintain your self-esteem.

If you feel that the criticism is unjustified then say so. When we say what we mean we are responding creatively. In the example which we are using I might reply, 'I don't think I am insensitive' or 'No, I don't accept that description of my behaviour'. Say what you feel clearly and convincingly. When we are high in self-esteem we behave creatively and this means taking responsibility for our own strengths and weaknesses. If the glove fits, then wear it. In other words, recognize and accept justified criticism: it is in your own best interests to do so. If it doesn't fit, don't try to own it. Stand up for yourself without attributing any blame.

Summary of Effective Ways to Deal With Criticism

- Learn to give constructive feedback instead of criticism and so help to break the chain of learned negatively reinforcing behaviour.

- Keep remembering that when you are being criticized you need not be victimized. Recognize that your internal critic supports your powerless child – both are just a set of negative beliefs, and beliefs can be changed.

- Apply the space-giving techniques as soon as you feel threatened. Use your witness to de-mystify your helplessness. Follow up with the affirmations: 'I love and value myself' and 'It's OK for me to make mistakes'.

- When you no longer feel threatened, evaluate the criticism. Accept it if it is justified – 'Yes I did make a mistake' – all the time remembering that making mistakes is part of learning. Refuse to accept unjustified criticism: 'No I certainly didn't behave in that way.' Whichever you do, ensure that your declaration is assertive – this is a creative and non-victimized response.

- Get to know your own strengths and weaknesses – self knowledge is a great protector. Who knows you better than you know yourself? Increase your self awareness by asking for constructive feedback: 'Do you think I was insensitive on that occasion?'

The more you practise these techniques the easier they will become. When you are able to separate yourself from your behaviour you can recognize your intrinsic self worth.

When you truly understand that you are lovable, valuable and worthy, then you have learned to create self-esteem.

And So We Can Break the Pattern

We have seen that learned negative self beliefs create low self-esteem. In this book we have looked at many techniques which can help us to let go of our negative beliefs. We now know how to change our beliefs so that we can respond creatively and really 'make things happen' in our lives. When we change our beliefs we change our behaviour and so we break our negative behaviour patterns.

The critical labelling of children ensures continued generations of people who are confused and unsure of themselves. Invalidated children grow into adults who have not received emotional support and so do not know how to give it. In this way the patterns of learned negative behaviour are passed from generation to generation.

Learning to give constructive feedback helps to break the cycle of negative, learned self beliefs. We came trailing clouds of glory and we came full of self-esteem and there is no reason why we have to lose these gifts. *Break the pattern.*

- Validate yourself
- Validate your children
- Validate each other.

Self-esteem is for everyone – it is our birthright.

Conclusion

Will the Real Me Stand Up

This book has been all about the ways in which self-esteem can be developed. As you work on the techniques which are appropriate for you, it is highly probable that you will discover that *you are not the person who you thought you were.* When the real you stands up you may get a surprise!

We have seen the way that negative self beliefs can create blocks to our freely flowing energy. When this happens we become out of balance because our mind, body, spirit and emotions are no longer operating in harmony and so we are low in self-esteem.

When we can change our negative beliefs about ourselves and the world, we change the quality of our lives. This change has a domino effect: as we learn ways to increase our self-esteem we also enhance the lives of others.

The real you is high in self-esteem. You are not a victim of circumstances. You have taken control of your life and you know how to respond creatively in any situation. 'What happens to you' is not as important as how you react to what happens. As you learn to love and respect yourself, your whole life changes. When you are able to validate yourself you become free to give emotional support to others. Our world has abundant resources. There will *always* be enough love and respect for everyone. *Love and respect are infinite resources.*

When there is mutual respect everyone feels self respect and so there is mutual self-esteem.

The way we treat the earth's resources and its inhabitants is a reflection of the way we treat ourselves. When we all learn to love and value ourselves there will be a global transformation!

Let the real me stand up and join hands with all the other real people. Together we can change our world.

Change yourself to change the world.

References and Further Reading

Burley-Allen, Madelyn   *Managing Assertively*, John Wiley and Sons Inc, 1983.

Dickson, Anne   *A Woman In Your Own Right*, Quartet Books Ltd, 1985.

Dyer, Dr Wayne W.   *Pulling Your Own Strings*, Hamlyn Books, 1979.

Fuglesang, Andreas   *About Understanding*, Dag Hammarskjold Foundation, 1982.

Gawain, Shakti   *Living In The Light*, Eden Grove Editions, 1988.

Hay, Louise L.   *You Can Heal Your Life*, Eden Grove Editions, 1988.

Norwood, Robin   *Women Who Love Too Much*, Arrow Books, 1985.

Orbach, Susie   'Feeling Our Way Through', *Weekend Guardian*, 23–4 Feb 1991.

Remember Be Here Now, Hanuman Foundation, 1980.

Satir, Virginia   *Peoplemaking*, Souvenir Press, 1978.

Index